15 days
of prayer with
JEAN-CLAUDE COLIN

15 days
of prayer/series

On a journey, it's good to have a guide. Even great saints took spiritual directors or confessors with them on their itineraries toward sanctity. Now you can be guided by the most influential spiritual figures of all time. The 15 Days of Prayer series introduces their deepest and most personal thoughts.

This popular series is perfect if you are looking for a gift, or if you want to be introduced to a particular guide and his or her spirituality. Each volume contains:

- ∝ A brief biography of the saint or spiritual leader
- ∝ A guide to creating a format for prayer or retreat
- ∝ Fifteen meditation sessions with focus points and reflection guides

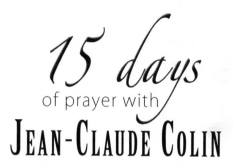

15 days
of prayer with
JEAN-CLAUDE COLIN

FRANÇOIS DROUILLY, S.M.

TRANSLATED BY
PHILIP GAGE, S.M.

NEW CITY PRESS
Hyde Park, NY

Published in the United States by New City Press
202 Comforter Blvd., Hyde Park, NY 12538
www.newcitypress.com
©2012 New City Press (English translation)

This book is a translation of *Prier 15 Jours Avec Jean-Claude Colin*,
published by Nouvelle Cité, 2010, Montrouge, France

Cover design by Durva Correia

Library of Congress Cataloging-in-Publication Data

Drouilly, François.
  [Prier 15 jours avec Jean-Claude Colin. English]
  15 days of prayer with Jean-Claude Colin / François Drouilly ;
translated by Philip Gage.
          p. cm.
  Includes bibliographical references (p.   ).
  ISBN 978-1-56548-435-1 (pbk. : alk. paper)
  1. Colin, Jean-Claude, 1790-1875--Meditations. 2. Mary, Blessed
Virgin, Saint--Devotion to. 3. Marist Fathers--Spiritual life.
4. Spiritual life--Catholic Church. I. Title.
BX4705.C687.D7613 2011
269'.6--dc23
                              2011041531

Printed in the United States of America

Contents

How to Use
This Book

*A*n old Chinese proverb, or at least what I am able to recall of what is supposed to be an old Chinese proverb, goes something like this: "Even a journey of a thousand miles begins with a single step." When you think about it, the truth of the proverb is obvious. It is impossible to begin any project, let alone a journey, without taking the first step. I think it might also be true, although I cannot recall if another Chinese proverb says it, "that the first step is often the hardest." Or, as someone else once observed, "the distance between a thought and the corresponding action needed to implement the idea takes the most energy." I don't know who shared that perception with me but I am certain it was not an old Chinese master!

With this ancient proverbial wisdom, and the not-so-ancient wisdom of an unknown contemporary sage still fresh, we move from proverbs to presumptions. How do these relate to the task before us?

I am presuming that if you are reading this introduction it is because you are contemplating a journey. My presumption is that you are preparing for a spiritual journey and that you have taken at least some of the first steps necessary to prepare for this journey. I also presume, and please excuse me if I am making too many presumptions, that in your preparation for the spiritual journey you have determined that you need a guide. From deep within the recesses of your deepest self, there was something that called you to consider Jean-Claude Colin as a potential companion. If my presumptions are correct, may I congratulate you on this decision? I think you have made a wise choice, a choice that can be confirmed by yet another source of wisdom, the wisdom that comes from practical experience.

Even an informal poll of experienced travelers will reveal a common opinion: it is very difficult to travel alone. Some might observe that it is even foolish. Still others may be even stronger in their opinion and go so far as to insist that it is necessary to have a guide, especially when you are traveling into uncharted waters and into territory that you have not yet experienced. I am of the personal opinion that a traveling companion is welcome under all circumstances. The thought of traveling alone, to some exciting destination without someone to share the journey with does not capture my imagination or channel my enthusiasm. However, with that being noted, what is simply a matter of preference on the normal journey becomes a matter of necessity when a person embarks on a spiritual journey.

The spiritual journey, which can be the most challenging of all journeys, is experienced best with a guide, a companion, or at the very least, a friend in whom you have placed your trust. This observation is not a preference or an opinion but rather an established spiritual necessity. All of the great saints with whom I am familiar had a spiritual director or a confessor who journeyed with them. Admittedly, at times the saints might well have traveled far beyond the experience of their guide and companion but more often than not they would return to their director and reflect on their experience. Understood in this sense, the director and companion provided a valuable contribution and necessary resource. When I was learning how to pray (a necessity for anyone who desires to be a full-time and public "religious person"), the community of men that I belong to gave me a great gift. Between my second and third year in college, I was given a one-year sabbatical, with all expenses paid and all of my personal needs met. This period of time was called novitiate. I was officially designated as a novice, a beginner in the spiritual journey, and I was assigned a "master," a person who was willing to lead me. In addition to the master, I was provided with every imaginable book and any other resource that I could possibly need. Even with all that I was provided, I did not learn how to pray because of the books and the unlimited resources, rather it was the master, the companion who was the key to the experience.

One day, after about three months of reading, of quiet and solitude, and of practicing all of the methods and descriptions of prayer that were available to me, the master called. "Put away the books, forget the method, and just listen." We went into a room, became quiet, and tried to recall the presence of God, and then, the master simply prayed out loud and permitted me to listen to his prayer. As he prayed, he revealed his hopes, his dreams, his struggles, his successes, and most of all, his relationship with God. I discovered as I listened that his prayer was deeply intimate but most of all it was self-revealing. As I learned about him, I was led through his life experience to the place where God dwells. At that moment I was able to understand a little bit about what I was supposed to do if I really wanted to pray.

The dynamic of what happened when the master called, invited me to listen, and then revealed his innermost self to me as he communicated with God in prayer, was important.

It wasn't so much that the master was trying to reveal to me what needed to be said; he was not inviting me to pray with the same words that he used, but rather that he was trying to bring me to that place within myself where prayer becomes possible. That place, a place of intimacy and of self-awareness, was a necessary stop on the journey and it was a place that I needed to be led to. I could not have easily discovered it on my own.

The purpose of the volume that you hold in your hand is to lead you, over a period of fifteen days or, maybe more realistically, fifteen prayer periods, to a place where prayer is possible. If you already have a regular experience and practice of prayer, perhaps this volume can help lead you to a deeper place, a more intimate relationship with the Lord.

It is important to note that the purpose of this book is not to lead you to a better relationship with Jean-Claude Colin, your spiritual companion. Although your companion will invite you to share some of his deepest and most intimate thoughts, your companion is doing so only to bring you to that place where God dwells. After all, the true measurement of all companions for the journey is that they bring you to the place where you need to be, and then they step back, out of the picture. A guide who brings you to the desired destination and then sticks around is a very unwelcome guest!

Many times I have found myself attracted to a particular idea or method for accomplishing a task, only to discover that what seemed to be inviting and helpful possessed too many details. All of my energy went to the mastery of the details and I soon lost my enthusiasm. In each instance, the book that seemed so promising ended up on my bookshelf, gathering dust. I can assure you, it is not our intention that this book end up in your bookcase, filled with promise, but unable to deliver.

There are three simple rules that need to be followed in order to use this book with a measure of satisfaction.

Place: It is important that you choose a place for reading that provides the necessary atmosphere for reflection and that does not allow for too many distractions. Whatever place you choose needs to be comfortable, have the necessary lighting, and, finally, have a sense of "welcoming" about it. You need to be able to look forward to the experience of the journey. Don't travel steerage if you know you will be more comfortable in first class and if the choice is realistic for you. On the other hand, if first class is a distraction and you feel more comfortable and more yourself in steerage, then it is in steerage that you belong.

My favorite place is an overstuffed and comfortable chair in my bedroom. There is a light over my shoulder, and the chair reclines if I feel a need to recline. Once in a while, I get lucky and the sun comes through my window and bathes the entire room in light. I have other options and other places that are available to me but this is the place that I prefer.

Time: Choose a time during the day when you are most alert and when you are most receptive to reflection, meditation, and prayer. The time that you choose is an essential component. If you are a morning person, for example, you should choose a time that is in the morning. If you are more alert in the afternoon, choose an afternoon time slot; and if evening is your preference, then by all means choose the evening. Try to avoid "peak" periods in your daily routine when you know that you might be disturbed. The time that you choose needs to be your time and needs to work for you.

It is also important that you choose how much time you will spend with your companion each day. For some it will be possible to set aside enough time in order to read and reflect on all the material that is offered for a given day. For others, it might not be possible to devote one time to the suggested material for the day, so the prayer period may need to be extended for two, three, or even more sessions. It is not important how long it takes you; it is only important that it works for you and that you remain committed to that which is possible.

Freedom: It may seem strange to suggest that freedom is the third necessary ingredient, but I have discovered that it is most important. By freedom I understand a certain "stance toward life," a "permission to be myself and to be gentle and understanding of who I am." I am constantly amazed at how the human person so easily sets himself or herself up for disappointment and perceived failure. We so easily make judgments about ourselves and our actions and our choices, and very often those judgments are negative, and not at all helpful.

For instance, what does it really matter if I have chosen a place and a time, and I have missed both the place and the time for three days in a row? What does it matter if I have chosen, in that twilight time before I am completely awake and still a little sleepy, to roll over and to sleep for fifteen minutes more? Does it mean that I am not serious about the journey, that I really don't want to pray, that I am just fooling myself when I say that my prayer time is important to me? Perhaps, but I prefer to believe that it simply means that I am tired and I just wanted a little more sleep. It doesn't mean anything more than that. However, if I make it mean more than that, then I can become discouraged, frustrated, and put myself into a state where I might more easily give up. "What's the use? I might as well forget all about it."

The same sense of freedom applies to the reading and the praying of this text. If I do not find the introduction to each day helpful, I don't need to read it. If I find the questions for reflection at the end of the appointed day repetitive, then I should choose to close the book and go my own way. Even if I discover that the reflection offered for the day is not the one that I prefer and that the one for the next day seems more inviting, then by all means, go on to the one for the next day.

That's it! If you apply these simple rules to your journey you should receive the maximum benefit and you will soon find yourself at your destination. But be prepared to be surprised. If you have never been on a spiritual journey you should know that the "travel brochures" and the other descriptions that you might have heard are nothing compared to the real thing. There is so much more than you can imagine.

A final prayer of blessing suggests itself:

> Lord, catch me off guard today.
> Surprise me with some moment of
>   beauty or pain
> So that at least for the moment
> I may be startled into seeing that you
>   are here in all your splendor,
> Always and everywhere,

Barely hidden,
Beneath,
Beyond,
Within this life I breathe.

Frederick Buechner

Rev. Thomas M. Santa, CSsR
Liguori, Missouri

Historical Overview
Jean-Claude Colin
(1790–1875)

*J*ean-Claude Colin was born in 1790 in the village of Saint-Bonnet-le-Troncy in the Loire region of southeastern France. He was the eighth and last child of a rather well-off farming family. In 1816 at the age of twenty-six years he was ordained a priest. Between these two dates, the world changed.

Times are hard

The French Revolution had overturned all the foundational institutions and had destroyed the very bases of a regime in force already for ten centuries. The "divine right" monarchy was guillotined with King Louis XVI. Religion was undermined from within with the obligation for priests to swear an oath of loyalty to the national (or "constitutional") Church. Monastic and religious orders were banned for being opposed to personal freedom. Grievous consequences followed for those who refused to obey the new laws: they were hunted down and suffered public denunciations, deportations, imprisonment, and persecution. To avoid these punishments, some citizens took the initiative and fled into exile. Among the various indignities done to the Church, we should also note the confiscation of ecclesiastical property, declared by the new government to be national property and available for sale to the public. Previous moral teaching and practice were shattered when the revolutionary government authorized divorce, based on nothing more than mutual consent. The most ruthless of the revolutionaries went so far as to try to eradicate all traces of Christianity with measures that were totally incomprehensible to the simple people: suppressing the names of saints in everyday life (names of villages, towns, streets, rivers, etc.), replacing the familiar calendar with a new secular one, the attempt to establish the new worship of a "Supreme Being," and often the abandonment, if not the outright destruction, of existing worship spaces.

The hardest of all, perhaps, was warfare, constant and everywhere, in France, on the borders, abroad, or among the French themselves, between different provinces, or with Napoleon in the whole of Europe, from Moscow to Madrid. In the wake of all this, we find so much destruction — moral, economic, and social.

And for young men, they faced the threat of military conscription, that is, being drafted into the army. One way to get out of going to the army was to pay a "replacement" if you had the money. Many preferred to risk desertion. One of those was Jean-Marie Vianney, future companion of Colin in the major seminary and the future Curé of Ars. In making this choice, he wondered if one was required to obey an emperor who had imprisoned the pope.

Jean-Claude Colin went through all that. He did not see what might appear to others as "social advancement" or "progress." No, for him the world was evil. His was an age of excess and ignorance. In the country area where he grew up, the Loire, his own father had been pursued by the police for helping the parish priest, who refused to honor the new laws, hide in the nearby woods. Both his mother and his father were deeply affected by the turmoil. They both died in 1795, three weeks apart from each other. Jean-Claude was five years old. At the age of seven, he attended several clandestine Masses celebrated at night and in barns for fear of reprisal.

He was a pious, interior and meditative boy. His pastor encouraged him to enter the seminary. He wanted to very much, but he was apprehensive about actually being a priest. Who could blame him?

Ordained a priest in 1816

The young men whom Colin met at the seminary in Lyons a few years later had all experienced the same upheavals brought by the Revolution. They would have certainly endorsed the observations of the church historian, André Latreille, who titled two chapters of his book on this period, "1799, the Destruction of the Catholic Church," and "1814, the Desolation of the Catholic Church."[a]

Even if we recognize historically that "de-Christianization" began in France before the Revolution, nevertheless, the ordeal was terrible. It was in this oppressive context and climate that the young men were going to be ordained priests in 1816, preparing to work in an unrecognizable Church. They would become part of an aging, decimated and impoverished clergy. Many priests who had earlier gotten married had already now abandoned the ministry. There was no lack of ongoing disputes between "faithful" priests and those who approved and signed the civil constitution for the clergy, the so-called "swearers of the oath." These young priests would often be sent to churches and parishes

---

a. André Latreille (1901-1984) Prize-winning historian and history professor teaching in both France and Canada, specializing in church history. His book, *L'Eglise catholique et la Révolution française* ["The Catholic Church and the French Revolution"], appeared in 1946. [Translator's note]

was no lack of ongoing disputes between "faith-ful" priests and those who approved and signed the civil constitution for the clergy, the so-called "swearers of the oath." These young priests would often be sent to churches and parishes that had been poorly maintained, if not com-pletely ravaged in the course of the upheavals. We can easily imagine their plans, their fervent intentions and, no doubt, their apprehension over the struggles they would be facing.

In this atmosphere, one of the young semi-narians, Jean-Claude Courveille, recounted for his closest companions, but in guarded words, a "revelation" he had in his home town of Le Puy. The Blessed Virgin allowed him to glimpse into the future to a group of religious men who would pick up the torch dropped by the Jesuits (they had been banished from France) and they would bear the name of Mary, in distinction to the Jesuits who bear the name of Jesus. Is this a true revelation or an interior locution, or something else? No one will ever know any more than Courveille himself let on to them. But what is certain is the very strong link which he established between the experience he had and Mary's "wish" for a society which would bear her name.

So, the seminarians share, they dream, they elaborate their plans, almost as if they were hatching a plot. And finally, the morning after

had prompted at its foundation a great re-flour-
ishing of the Church in the wake of Protestant
ruptures and reforms. "We irrevocably dedicate
ourselves and all our goods, in the fullest degree
we can, to the Society of the blessed Virgin."
(EK 145)

On the ground

After the Fourvière pledge came the reality
of being "on the ground" in their new assign-
ments that they had to take up. At that point,
they were still diocesan priests called by their
respective bishops to serve in the diocese, and
they were, accordingly, spread out far from
one another. At the start of his first assignment at the parish in Cerdon, a small town in
the Department of Ain, Colin was somewhat
backed into a corner. On the one hand, he had
continued to ruminate over the project of a
religious society. On the other, in his various
"missions" in the country towns of the Bugey
mountain area, he began to meet those men
and women who had fully experienced both the
Revolution and the Empire and did not know
too well where things stood or how to recon-
nect with the Church which was now in such a
sorry state. We can easily imagine the settling
of scores he must have been involved with as
he met the townspeople, dealing notably with
all the different positions they might have had

about the Church, the pastor, the "national" church, etc. Later in 1829, Colin accepted the position of superior at the College in Belley. It was then that he had to confront the new generation of students, young people whose parents had experienced all the upheavals. Like their children, the parents were not easy to handle. Politics were brought inside the school: you were either for King Louis-Philippe or against him; you defended or you attacked the work and memory of the Emperor Napoleon! Here we have a generation of youth without a compass, according to the economist Saint-Simon,[a] who suggested that they might find guidance in a so-called "Gospel of the Iron Horse," since the Industrial Revolution was just dawning on the horizon. And somewhat later, Guizot[b] thought he would raise the level a bit by his provocative and exciting cry, "Go! Get rich!"

All these many experiences allowed Colin and his early companions to clarify and to test what it was like to live a life "in Mary's way."

a. Claude Henri de Rouvroy, Count of Saint-Simon (1760-1825) was a French philosopher and economist and an early socialist theorist. His social teaching came just before the Industrial Revolution and was one of the influences on the development of socialism. [Translator's note]
b. François Guizot (1787-1874) was a noted French historian, orator and statesman. [Translator's note]

The Marist project on the way to its achievement

The only thing still left for the group to become a religious congregation at this point was the approval of Pope Gregory XVI. Once they had that, they could come together from their individual dioceses; they could freely define and organize their ministries, independent now from any diocesan oversight. Such papal recognition came in 1836. At that time Rome needed missionaries to evangelize people living on the many islands of the South Pacific. It was far away. It would be hard. There were many risks involved. Colin stepped up to the challenge and sent the first Marist missionaries. One of those in the first band was St. Peter Chanel, who left in 1836 and was eventually assassinated, a martyr, on the island of Futuna in 1841.

So Colin became the superior general of a religious congregation, the Society of Mary. He continued as general until 1854. Father Marcellin Champagnat, who was himself also a Marist priest, founded and developed the congregation of Marist teaching Brothers, as he was always so passionate and concerned about the education of children living in remote, country places.

From the very beginning of the Marist venture, women helped the priests, like the young lady, Jeanne-Marie Chavoin. She was the first, then was joined by other eager volunteers.

Slowly and often with hardship, these women gained autonomy and defined their own mission, eventually becoming a separate congregation in the Marist family, the Marist Sisters.

Finally, a laywoman from Lyons, Françoise Perroton, almost fifty years old and deeply attracted to the foreign missions, made her decision to answer the call of some women on the island of Ouvea in the South Pacific. She left, by herself. After years of difficulties, some other French women joined her, and these missionary sisters became yet another branch of the Marist Family, the Missionary Sisters of the Society of Mary.

As for Colin, he was trying to respond to multiple requests for missionaries to go to the Pacific, but also to many requests to open or take over schools in France and to send priests to parish missions and renewals in cities or in the countryside. He was working at the same time to finish the rule of life for the Marist congregation. The results are undeniably impressive. When Colin left office in 1854, he had sent 74 Marist priests to Oceania, 26 Little Brothers of Mary (from Champagnat's group), and 17 coadjutor brothers (from the Fathers' group). Back in France, he had accepted the administration of six schools.

Colin spent the last years of his life at La Neylière, a peaceful residence in the hill country south of Lyons. He worked there in his retirement quite diligently to bring final shape to a Marist lay "branch" which he had been pondering since the very beginning. He died in 1875.

Invitation to
the Journey

*C*olin's spiritual experience did not spring from his head full-formed. It came as the result of his encounter, which was sometimes painful, with the world in which he was born and raised. It also drew on the personal disclosures that his companion Jean-Claude Courveille confided to him concerning Mary's name and her active presence at the birth of the Church.

Starting with that, we can design a plan for our prayer. First of all, *to lay the foundations,* which are tasting God, bearing a name, and drawing near to the source again as we contemplate the early Church.

Secondly, *the spiritual attitudes* which flow from these foundations stand as a critique of the way the Church had interacted with the Ancien Régime:[a] the practice of the hidden life, mod-

---

a. "Earlier Order," a term referring to the ensemble of monarchy, aristocracy, government, church and society, which functioned in the centuries before the French Revolution (1789-1799). One of the aims of the Revolution was to abolish the *"Ancien Régime."* [Translator's note]

esty, the references to Nazareth, with that rather original take on "holy cheerfulness." (After so many setbacks, cheerfulness was undoubtedly truly needed.)

Next come the *desired behaviors* "on the ground" with real people as they are. Again, these seem to us to be extremely timely: rejecting cupidity, living somehow unknown and hidden, and, even more, practicing mercy always and everywhere.

And finally, *the horizon widens*: the Church is not limited to this handful of Marist religious or to their being implanted in several countries. Mary invites us to look farther and wider. Colin draws everyone to the world's farthest ends, into a Church which will finally recover the fresh perfection of her beginnings.

Abbreviations

C   Constitutions of the Society of Mary, 1988.

Colin.sup   *Documents pour l'étude du généralat de J.-Claude Colin (1836–1854).* Four volumes of archival documents, mostly from the pen of Jean-Claude Colin during his term as superior general. Edited by Charles Girard Marist Publications, Rome, 2010.

EK   *A Book of Texts, for the study of Marist spirituality,* compiled by Edwin Keel. Center for Marist Studies, Rome, 1993.

FA   *A Founder Acts, reminiscences of Jean-Claude Colin by Gabriel-Claude Mayet.* Marist Publications, Rome, 1983.

FS   *A Founder Speaks, spiritual talks of Jean-Claude Colin.* Marist Publications, Rome, 1975.

LM   *Lay Marists, anthology of historical sources,* edited by Charles Girard. Marist Publications, Rome, 1993.

OM   *Origines maristes (1786–1836).* Four volumes of archival and historical documents, edited by Jean Coste and Gaston Lessard. Marist Publications, Rome, 1960.

1
Tasting God

Focus Point

///////////////

Saints, mystics and spiritual writers have tried to find words to convey the reality of an experience that essentially refuses to be reduced to human words. "Meeting God," "being surprised by God," "falling into God's embrace," etc. have been suggested. Some few have offered "touching God." Father Colin is among the very few to rely on the metaphor "tasting God." As we will see for Day 1, "tasting" is an immensely rich image and uniquely appropriate for the Marist experience.

///////////////

If I were in charge [of the novices], I would try simply to unite them to God, to bring them to a spirit of prayer. When the good Lord dwells in the heart, it is he who sets everything in motion. Without that, everything that you do is completely useless; no mat-

ter how you plant the seed and tire yourself out, the life-giving principle is still lacking. But having once tasted God, a novice will turn to him again and again. It is a treasure in his soul, something to which he is constantly brought back as to his own center. There he will love to converse with God. (FS 63:2)

///////////

" *Tasting God.*" This expression runs all through Fr. Colin's life. He mentions it to young men drawn to Marist life. He repeats it to the older men during retreats or gatherings. He recalls it to missionaries embarking for Oceania. And it is always with the same insistence. It is a prerequisite, a foundational experience, the cornerstone which fears neither the wear and tear of time nor the raging storm. The experience of tasting God has for Colin the importance of all or nothing. Without it, we build on sand. But anyone who has experienced it can make great progress. He can count on reaching his goal.

But this is not a magic formula. Tasting God seems more like the expression of a first encounter, even if it eventually fades! It is something like a lightning bolt. You can come away from it with "your heart wounded," Colin once said. Think of lovers as they reminisce. "That day something happened, and it's in my memory and my heart for the rest of my life. That day,

I knew that I loved you. That day, I knew that you loved me. That day, someone looked at me and I discovered in their eyes that I was worth something, that I counted. And now the seasons have come and gone; and trials have come my way. But in fair weather or in the howling storm, I can still recall, still relive, that moment, and I am convinced that it was not a dream."

Is this really for me?

Is this really for the run-of-the-mill mortal being? Isn't it an experience reserved for those on a high spiritual plane? Is it not precisely for future religious?

Colin would have to smile at that idea, thinking of his first companions and of himself as well. Really, these simple young men, coming most often from their rural backgrounds, hardly looked like the desert Fathers and even less like experts in the sacred sciences! Up to that point, not one of them could report having had a transport of spiritual ecstasy. To tell the truth, they looked just like most of us, and they certainly shared with us all our own mediocrities:

- ∞ distractions at prayer, which turn into boredom if we let them continue
- ∞ the sense of dryness: "what should I say, what should I do?"
- ∞ the sense of time wasted whenever we start going over in our minds all the things we need

to do, all the work that awaits us on our desk, in the house, etc.

And then there's the sense of weariness that comes from evaluating our efforts and finding appalling results: "I've prayed so much and yet nothing has changed." And who cannot count all the experiences of discouragement that follow a failure of some kind, or a personal or family crisis, that result in the urge to simply let everything drop? We all experience every one of these things.

Tasting God — is that really for me?

An experience rather than a method

First of all, tasting God is a gift from God. It is not something that we can achieve by our own merits or our own efforts. It comes by grace alone. In that sense, there is no "method" for reaching it. Today, of course, we are offered so many methods (and there were even more in Colin's time): reciting a *mantra* or repeating a special formula, concentrating on our breathing, and other forms of meditation. This is not to belittle all those practices. How wonderful if any of them prove to be helpful to us. But let us be clear that none of those activities will bring us to taste God.

Tasting God is also not the result of our learning or our reading, whether theological, spiritual, etc. One way of saying this is that we do not taste God with our mind!

But neither do we taste God only with our heart. Using the very word "taste" opens for us so obviously an experience of the senses. Yet, at the same time Colin invites us to avoid the idea of fleeting emotions, pious enthusiasms, feelings of happiness which can so easily vanish as soon as they show up, leaving us somewhat more bewildered than we were before. After all, in the course of purification there comes the occasional time of absence.

To taste God requires that we take time for him and prepare ourselves for the experience. Ask a great sommelier how he goes about appreciating a superb wine. Does he taste it just anywhere, at any old time, while he is watching television? Of course not. It takes time, attention, and clearly it also takes patience to find exactly what he is looking for, exactly what he is hoping to discover.

To taste God is to be nourished by him. And this happens to us more frequently than we think. To find that a word from God has "taste" is to recognize that it is delectable, that it gives flavor to my life and to life itself, and that it enhances life. It enhances our horizons. Suppose there is a Scripture passage that I have heard several dozen times or more, so I naturally think I know it by heart. Yet just today (why do these things happen?) one word touched me, moved me, as if it had been placed there precisely for me!

That good taste which comes from an encounter where, for the first time in a long time, I could say what I thought I should have said, or I could hear what I have been waiting to hear: forgiveness (either given or received), words of trust or truth, or words of confidence and intimacy. I come away from such an encounter stronger, with a taste of peace of mind and heart.

The Gospel helps us understand the power of this expression, "tasting God." When some villagers were intrigued by Jesus, who began to show up in the midst of the people and perhaps after hearing him once or twice, they became bold enough to dare to ask him, "Where do you stay?" Jesus' answer is not complicated. "Come and you will see." John quickly ends the passage, "So they went to see where he was lodged, and stayed with him that day." That was enough to set the direction for their whole life, enough to convince them for the rest of their life. They tasted a moment of intimacy with Jesus. They kept that moment alive in their hearts, and they constantly came back to it.

With all trust

Colin invites *us* to the same experience. We understand pretty well that it will not always be for us as awesome as it was for the first disciples. But at any moment of our lives we can make ourselves available to the Lord. That would suppose perhaps that for once we put aside the long list of our concerns, our wants, our worries, our regrets, not to mention the list of our sins. Let us put aside our fear of emptiness. Let us take time for silence then. Let us go back to the words of a familiar prayer or psalm text and take the time to savor it. Or again, let us recall just one of the times that we have already tasted God and thank him for how good it was. My trust in God will allow him to continue to act and make my life flourish.

> Keep my soul in peace,
> Your law, O Lord, is my delight.
> I take my rest in you, O Lord.
> Yes, when we have tasted God, truly,
>   we keep going back to him.

Reflection Questions

Can you remember "tasting" God in the past? What were the circumstances? Liturgy? Some other sacrament? Private prayer? Encountering another person? Reading? What would be the best actions and attitudes at the present time to prepare you to "taste" God? While not necessarily committing yourself to do *more* or pray *more*, what changes or improvements can you adopt in your present life to allow God to come in and for you to "taste" God?

2
Bearing a Name

Focus Point

////////////

Many of us will remember from studying Scripture how powerful the concept of a person's name is. Moses almost had to wheedle it out of the Presence in the burning bush to reveal his name. We understand God's reluctance to do so, because if someone knows your name he has a certain power over you, and he can see into the mystery of your being. Also in the Bible, individuals receive a new name to indicate a new mission: Jacob to Israel, Simon to Peter, Saul to Paul. In Day 2, we reflect more deeply on the mystery of Mary's name and on Fr. Colin's approach to that mystery. Those who join Mary's religious family come to understand that it was really Mary who called them and she gave them her own name to be their name now. "Marist" at the end of someone's name may not represent a legal change, but

it does truly stand for the spiritual reality that
"Mary" is now my last name.

/////////////

*What have we to fear? The blessed Virgin is lead-
ing us. She is saying to us, "I am marching ahead of
you." Gentlemen, given that thought — the blessed
Virgin is marching with me — who would not feel
full of courage and of confidence in any trial? And
then, if I reflect on the name I bear, what a source
of hope, of reassurance! But the name is no longer
enough. For I profess to belong to Mary, and I want
to profess my belonging to her even more. I want my
devotion to her to redouble, that my dependence on
her be total and continual. I shall always hold her by
the hand. In my troubles, in my difficulties, I shall
say to her, "Blessed Virgin, help me, I falter. I cast my
self into your merciful lap, help me to pick myself up
again." (FS, 176)*

/////////////

A name held in reserve

*R*ight from the beginning of the Marist venture, Colin was convinced that the choice
of Mary's name for this new religious family was
not an accident. The name was "held in reserve,"
since no other congregation had ever taken it
before, he tells us. And yet there was no lack of
Marian congregations at that time; in fact, they

were proliferating. But these groups fell under the title of a particular mystery or some devotion to Mary: Our Lady of Sorrows, the Immaculate Conception, Immaculate Heart of Mary, etc. But as for the very name itself of Mary, only the Marists bear it. Eventually Colin will certainly have some difficulty with the existence of Fr. Guillaume Chaminade's religious order of "Marianists." "But they came after," he would say with relief.

> *The name of Mary that we bear was not*
> *   given us by men;*
> *it came to us from heaven.* (EK, 284)

But after these thoughts on the mysterious origins, let us return to a very simple reality which is open to everyone. To bear Mary's name (to put it that simply) is to go back to the woman of the Gospel, to the few words reported about her, to a few attitudes and a few scenes. That's all there is. But that's a great deal, because it is the person of Mary that counts. Marists are called to live the adventure with her. Colin says it in his own way:

> *The name does not matter; the reality does.*
> (EK, 282) *These are riches we hold in our*
> *soul. It is truly a treasure!*

Hence, our relationship with Mary does not follow the lines of devotion, any more than it comes from contemplating one or another mystery in Mary's life. Neither does Colin invite us to "imitate" Mary. When he uses that word he does it particularly to highlight the paradox between her status as "Mother of God" and the humility of her life. On all these issues Colin remains subtle, since he is not really passing on to Marists a deep Mariological content. Personally, he showed no special interest in the many Marian apparitions that took place during his lifetime. No, what counts for him is a connection to her as a person. This name that we bear is so important to Colin that he chose to make "the Most Holy Name of Mary" the patronal feast of the congregation.

Caution against childishness

"O holy Mary, we are your children, you are our mother." This is how a consecration to Our Blessed Lady would typically begin. *"Yes, I will always take her by the hand."* Colin wrote about Mary. We believe that Mary has made a free and reciprocal choice of those men and women who answer her call. Does that mean they must be like well behaved grown-up children clinging to their Mama? Is this a choice or is it dependency?

Colin and his first companions found themselves in a situation where they could not entertain any delusions. Mary's name was not a magic charm that allowed them to resolve whatever problem they faced. And if they needed to prove their "devotion" or "dependence," it was not so that they could stay snug and secure in her family. Rather, it was to follow Mary in complete freedom and responsibility, totally convinced that she was not there to take their place and do their work for them.

She would do all that *with* them, at their side, as their leader, like an army general ("under her banner"). Colin does not bequeath any particular method to us, but rather a way of being and living. He invites us to work in the "depths" or at the "center" of our being. And there we will find Mary as the source of our commitment, the source of our existence. This is not at all in the sense that Mary takes the place of God. But, because Mary gave life to Jesus, she certainly knows how to bring him to birth and make him grow and act within us and through us. Her name which we bear is a call to go "toward Mary," that is, toward life.

Her name functions as a call or as a recall. Who among us has not at one time or another experienced emptiness, anxiety or frustration? Fatigue, discouragement, the sense of not being on top of things, of not changing and even more of not being able to change. Facing ourselves can become agony. And then Colin's words come back to us or, more basically perhaps, Gospel images come back to us: "The Lord has done great things for me, he has looked upon his servant in her low-liness." Or again: "Let it be done to me as you say, I am the handmaid of the Lord."

From that moment on, I am no longer on my own when challenged to ford the raging stream. Much more than the powerful woman who can obtain for us what we do not ourselves dare to ask the Lord, Mary reminds us who we are and that the Lord can do for us what he has done for her and for all those who recognize them-selves as the lowly. These are the ones who wait for him, trust him, hope in him and repeat her words, "I am the handmaid, I am the servant of the Lord." And also, "The Lord has done great things for me."

To enter a story

Binding himself firmly to Mary's name, Colin inscribed the adventure that he lived with his first companions in a story, the story of the annunciation and the coming of a savior for the world. Of course, Mary plays a major role in this story. But this story is never finished, since we can never quite finish a mission if we can never entirely finish responding to it. We must continue to pursue the task in each age and time according to their particular conditions. This was urgent for Colin. And he could find no bet-ter guide than the Blessed Virgin to bring it to completion. Or, to express it more exactly, it was entirely obvious to him that she was the one to complete the story.

The invitation is strong and encouraging. No doubt the mission remains difficult, but we are just links in the chain. Others have gone before us, and others will pick up where we leave off. But, above all, we are not alone. Mary works with us!

This insistence on "the name" invites me to dwell on the names that I bear — my Baptismal name, my Confirmation name, my family name, or whatever other names I have. Do I bear these names? Do I uphold these names? Do these names *bear me* up? Does it ever occur to me to be grateful for the name I bear?

And the name of Mary, where does it fit in with those questions? What relation does it inspire within me? Is it present in my faith journey? I need to remember that I can take up as totally my own, at any time, in whatever situation I happen to be, Mary's own words in her great thanksgiving hymn, the Magnificat, "My soul proclaims the glory of the Lord!"

Reflections Questions

Do you know the meaning or etymology of your names? Why did your parents give them to you? Do you like your names? Do they give you support or comfort? Do they have a special meaning for you? Many people choose a new name when they receive the sacrament of Confirmation. Have you ever chosen names for yourself? If you could choose your own names, what would they be and why? People deeply in love (parents towards children and *vice versa*, spouses, friends, etc.) often have private names of endearment and intimacy for each other. That seems only natural when we love others. Also, Scripture presents many symbolic and poetical names for God and for Jesus, like Rock, Stronghold, Shepherd, Bridegroom, Lamb, etc. What would be your intimate, personal name for God the Father, and for Jesus? What do you think is God's endearing name for you, his beloved child?

3
Mary at the Birth of the Church

Focus Point ///////////

It is surprising to discover how many founders and foundresses of religious orders throughout the ages all drew on the same scene in the Acts of the Apostles for the model of what they wanted their congregations to be: one in heart and soul, sharing in prayer, the breaking of the bread, material goods held in common, and the spreading of the Gospel. Whether in the 15th or 17th or 19th centuries, looking back to this ideal of the early Church community provided direction, motive, inspiration and consolation. Idealizing a past experience might possibly lead to promoting a fantasy or portraying a Utopia, especially if the daily reality in my own time and space proves to be mostly flaws, shortcomings and weakness. But that should never imply that we stop focusing on the hallowed origins and the holy promise of a better future. This becomes all the more true if we take on Fr. Colin's view of the new-born Church where Mary is, at the same time, our mother, our sister, and our companion on the pilgrim way.

//////////////

Gentlemen, that our Lord left the Blessed Virgin behind on earth after his Ascension is without doubt a great mystery. The apostles needed her to guide them, and to be in a sense the foundress of the Church. At the end of time her protection will shine forth in an even greater way.... She will make her presence felt even more than in the beginning. Let us therefore be filled with courage. Let us all have but one heart and one soul. Let us not like to have people speak of us. Let us imitate our mother: she did not have people speak of her, the Gospel only named her four times, and yet what good she did! (FS, 116, 7–8)

//////////////

The Utopian community

*C*olin would have us share his deep conviction that Mary was present at the foundation of the Church. She will also be there at the end of history. She fulfills this role with a mother's discretion. And those who bear her name are to imitate her.

Colin draws his inspiration from several sources. He took the revelation of Jean-Claude Courveille, his companion at the origins, and

added to it his reading of the seventeenth-cen-
tury mystic, Mary of Agreda, who described
the daily life and customs of the early Church.
This Spanish nun obtained knowledge from
her "visions." From these, Colin treasures the
memory of a Mary more hidden, more unob-
trusive than any of the apostles, placing herself
at their service, obedient to them, listening
to them like a simple disciple, making absolutely nothing of her position as Queen of the
Apostles or Mother of the Messiah, but truly
fitting right into the community.

Rereading these passages from a Marist
perspective takes us far beyond the category of
revelations and visions, yet it does not prevent
us at all from seeing this image as an "allusion"
that Luke makes in the Acts of the Apostles
(Acts 1:12–14). After the Resurrection, the
apostles sought safety in the upper room with
other disciples, some of them women, and one
of them, Mary. There were perhaps fifteen or
twenty people "united and devoted to constant
prayer." Mary is described as among the apostles and the brothers of Jesus. They are not two
rival factions but at least two groups, each of
which has reasons to claim to be the legitimate
heirs of the Savior. The apostles have been companions in good times and in bad, witnesses to
the words and deeds of Jesus, coming from
different horizons and origins, and all of them

ready to spread the good news, especially after the Holy Spirit comes upon them. But there are also Jesus' "brothers," which would be a good sized group of family members, whose interest is to insist on the Jewish tradition of the family. We know from Acts and from Paul's writings that these "nuances" of differences would later turn into rather serious conflicts between the factions, as was the case in the Council of Jerusalem concerning new Gentile converts and what exactly they were expected to observe of Jewish ritual. (Acts 15)

So, Mary is there, in their midst, seated among the brothers and the apostles. She bears in herself a double membership, she belongs to both groups. Physically, she is mother; spiritually, she is disciple. No doubt, she remembers the saying, the answer Jesus gave to those who told him that his family wanted to see him, "My mother and my brothers are those who hear the word of God and put it into practice" (Lk 8:19-21). She was there, and she was part of the one group and also part of the other. We can easily believe that not for nothing is Mary described as one in "unity of constant prayer" with those in the upper room.

Coming back to the real community

Colin finds his happiness in this scene. Here is Mary working in harmony with others, not calling attention to herself, without any show, without claims to any prestige. In her he finds material to reflect upon both for his religious family and for the Church of his times. That was a church riddled with distinct and strong tensions. It was not a question of Jewish ritual or how to observe the Law, but at that time the issue was between priests who had not sworn the Constitutional oath during the Revolution and who were now returning from exile only to look with disgust on their bishops, and all those others who had taken the oath and were now highly placed officials in their dioceses. There was also ill will generally among Christians and between Christians over this issue. In such a climate, how could anyone re-establish functioning church communities? Colin took on Mary's own discretion, encouraging his religious disciples to forsake all pretensions in favor of the common cause. Marists will be at the service of the bishops for whom they work. As they preach the country missions, there will be no attempt to outshine the parish priest, they will not get mixed up in parish gossip or have any relations with parishioners other than those regarding the mission itself. Marists work for the Gospel, not for themselves. Besides that, Colin considered unconditional allegiance to the pope to be the best defense against what history teaches us about the creation of "national churches," that a national church is always adrift and almost always destroys itself.

Is this a task that has to be constantly taken up again?

This is the unity which must be at the center of our Church — not to bring people to heel or to impose uniformity, but rather to promote that unity which is dear to the heart of Christ. What must we do to go beyond criticizing, distrust or simple herd-like acceptance? What must we do so that a parish does not appear to be a closed club but rather like a place of gathering for all Christians? What must we do so that communities with a more prophetic or charismatic bent are not suspected of being on the fringe or of living and working on their own? How can we bring together those who believe in active, zealous evangelization and those who live the humble witness of their ordinary lives more discreetly? How can we understand the nostalgia of some Church members whose experience comes from the Church of yesteryear where "everything was fine"? The list of friction points is endless, without counting today's trends of suspicion of the institution, suspicion of the official word, and the criticisms that sometimes come for both speaking too much and also not saying anything!

Mary does not show up with a readymade answer to these questions. She is, however, there, saying little, listening much to one and all, not resorting to arguments from authority or claiming to be the only one who can resolve the issue, and claiming even less to be the one who is right over everyone else. Her wish is that of any mother, that they all live and grow and flourish together.

I am certainly not responsible for everything that goes wrong in the Church! But, still, I can wonder about my attitude and my commitment in this task of unity. How do I admit the value of another person's word? How do I approach another unconditionally and with an intentionally positive attitude? How can I recognize the positive value of a point of view which is not my own? How can I avoid seeing myself automatically on the side of truth? How can I accept meeting people whose point of view I do not share and yet still working and sharing ideas with them?

Colin repeats over and over again that the Society of Mary has no other model than the Church at its birth. Our Church today, like that of the apostles, can live only in a unanimity among diverse groups not a uniformity or fusion of understanding. This unity includes complementarity, community prayer, and availability to the Holy Spirit. The Christian journey is definitely not a solitary path. We will all arrive together at our destination. With Mary.

Reflection Questions

On this Day 3, we have reflected on origins, particularly the origins of the Church. Were you ever part of the foundation or birth of a group, a club, an organization, etc.? What did you experience? Enthusiasm? Hope? Uncertainty? Solidarity with the other members? Do you have good memories from that time (or not)? Try to compare the origins of a group that you are familiar with (especially the Church) with its present-day situation. What events or attitudes from the beginnings should still guide the group? Are there things that should not be repeated? Things that should be avoided? Can you think of situations, difficulties, conflicts, etc., and of experiences of grace like progress, reconciliation, blessings, etc., where you feel that Mary is/was present? Can you name current situations where you would like Mary to be present?

4
Nazareth

Focus Point

////////////

Before Vatican II, one extremely widespread image of the Church and the World was that the world is so evil and menacing, eager to deceive and corrupt any decent Christian soul, that anyone who wanted to be saved should avoid the world, or according to an ancient spiritual formula, "flee the world." Monasteries and religious orders were explicitly designed to keep the world at bay, to wall out the evil and protect the refugee inside. In that context the image of Nazareth often stood for protection, isolation, hidden and interior prayer. How things have changed! Vatican II reminds all Christians, laity and religious as well, that they have heard the call to transform the *world* – yes, the *world*. They are to give the witness of their specifically different lives, rich with good works and prayer. *They* are the leaven called to transform the dough. Father Colin had this great insight. For him, Nazareth was precisely the place to meet

Mary and Jesus, to renew one's energy and enthusiasm. And *from within* the house at Nazareth, we can look out onto the world and see more clearly all those places in the world that need us, all those places where we can go and do real good.

//////////////

We must hold fast, my dear confreres, to the spirit which presided over the birth of the Society. Inquire further and further into it every day; you will only be good Marists insofar as you really put it into practice. And what is this spirit? It is the spirit of the Blessed Virgin, a spirit of modesty, of humility, of prudence, of simplicity, of discretion. In all things let us look to Mary, let us imitate her life at Nazareth. She did more than the apostles for the new-born Church; she is Queen of the apostles, but she did it without any stir, she did it above all by her prayers. Let us therefore unite silence and prayer with action. The Society of Mary desires that we, her children, should be missionaries of action and missionaries of prayer. (FS, 190)

//////////////

Nazareth, "a hole in the wall"

Nazareth and the new-born Church, prayer and action, silence and action, missionaries of prayer and missionaries of action — connecting all these together brings us directly in line with the spiritual pedagogy that Colin developed during the second part of his life.

Nazareth seemed to him a journey that every Marist must take. But Nazareth is a forgotten hole, "east of nowhere"! "Can anything good come out of it?" They say that Belley was like that. Nevertheless, the history of the Church begins at Nazareth. And the history of the Society of Mary begins at Belley. Jesus' life at Nazareth lasted for thirty years. That's ten times longer than his public life. Thirty years of Jesus' life during which, apparently, occurred only the ordinary everyday events of family life, a craftsman's daily tasks, the obscurity, the silence, and a normal life's negligible outcome. This was a time of formation, marked by obedience, apprenticeship, a kind of inactivity, discretion, and even self-renunciation. But Jesus lived throughout these thirty years in view of a future still fairly unclear, indeed unknown.

An anecdote might shed light on this intuition of Colin's. The story goes that Jean-Marie Vianney, Colin's friend at the seminary in Lyons, wanted to leave his parish in Ars on several occasions when he found himself exhausted and deeply discouraged. His desire was to take refuge at La Neylière, a property which Colin had acquired in the mountains south of Lyons. Colin said that while he was there he felt that he was at Nazareth. As it turned out, however, when the parishioners at Ars realized their pastor's plans, they would not let the Curé accomplish them. Even if this anecdote turns out to be partially legend, it sheds light on Colin's intuition. Nazareth was neither a cloister nor a hermitage. Colin was not seeking refuge there, and even less was he trying to hide out. What he did want was that someone could prepare himself there and resolve to live the Gospel before being sent to the farthest corners of the earth to share that Gospel with others.

Nazareth, a school of formation

Nazareth is a concept that can be of use to any Christian. It reminds us to guard against putting the cart before the horse. It tells us how spiritual life can tumble if it does not walk firmly on two solid feet, whether by inward withdrawal and prayer to flee the difficulties of living in the world, or by a generous but generally unproductive activity, when we are in the field and start to wonder, tired and discouraged, why we are working so hard and for whom. In Colin's time Marists in Oceania as well as in France knew the risks of becoming overburdened. In France, they were being asked to take over schools, parishes, places of pilgrimage, and in general to widen the scope of their mission.

So, considering time and place, what can Nazareth provide? Nothing, if we are speaking of content. Very much, however, if we just let ourselves get caught up in the mystery of Nazareth. After all, it is not simply nothing if you let yourself be shaped by the ordinariness of your days, by the quotidian of your life, to learn to look at work, familiar relationships, everyday meetings with others, etc., as the terrain where God waits for you, so that you can learn to live in the present moment, putting aside nostalgia for the past as well as projecting into the future. This is not the time to build castles in the air, even if they are castles for Oceania! This is the time for patience and silence. And for Colin, it is certain that the benefits that flow from this time will redound to anyone who is active and in the mission, and they will make him and his work fruitful and productive.

With Mary at Nazareth

So, will we give up everything for Nazareth? Not really. But we can at least take into consideration again those statements we find in St. Luke. "As for Mary, she treasured all these things and reflected on them in her heart" (2:19). "But they did not grasp what he [the twelve-year-old Jesus] said to them.... His mother meanwhile kept all these things in her heart" (2:50–51).

Mary attends to "these things," these events which happen to her. She welcomes them, but avoids questions, interpretations, or speculations. She doesn't look for the causes and doesn't imagine the consequences. She steers clear of turning in on herself or allowing anything personal to interfere with what has just happened. She projects none of her own hopes, none of her worries, none of her dreams. Rather, she gives her consent to reality. She does not go around the event, because the event reveals God to us! And it is being faithful to God to accept what is happening to us.

To stay at Nazareth, at least at one time or another, stands as a healing remedy for the mind and heart. It means making a deliberate choice to spend this time attentively. For most of our life we live in an atmosphere saturated with information, to such an extent that one fact vies for our attention over another, and we simply become indifferent to them all. In such a surrounding full of noise, words and messages, we can only hope to take the risk of silence, believing that out of it perhaps a "word" might just be born. Not one more word among all the million others, but a word of life.

To stay at Nazareth means to choose to "recollect," not only in the usual sense of devotion and respect for the places where we are. It also means to find yourself again, to find yourself present to yourself, casting aside any wish to make changes, find solutions or resolve problems. It means to surrender to another person, and to be able to say simply, in all truthfulness, "Here I am."

To come back to Nazareth means to remove yourself voluntarily from the grip of work, commitment and responsibility, to shut yourself off, for a time, from the incessant demands of everyday life. It means in some way to go back to square one to recover what is essential, agreeing to shed all your sensitivity, touchiness, self-satisfaction, and self-image. Take your bearings. Go back to the center. And from there, from Nazareth, find the path again that you must take to come out and reach out to others.

Nazareth is not a class to prepare us for contemplative life, and it is not a Zen session. It is a place for learning docility, fidelity to what God wants of us. It is where instruments for the Lord's service take shape.

There is not a moment to lose. Let us take the time to return to Nazareth. The decision will perhaps be painful, while reason, our daily duties, the commitments we've taken on will rise up to thwart us. But it will pay off! Look, we will be able to pick up our agendas and inbox messages later on. And, at that point we will be far more aware and much more free.

Reflection Questions

Have you ever found a place where you could find refuge, particularly spiritual refuge? What was it like? How did you feel there? How did you feel when it was time to leave? If you have not had much experience of a spiritual "refuge," what kind of place would be an ideal refuge for you? What would you be looking for? How would you want to feel there? Granted that the image of Nazareth remains mostly in our imagination and is not actually a geographical possibility for us, can you identify with any of the ideas we reflected on in Day 4? What is the value of returning, at least in our mind's eye, to that house in Galilee with Jesus and Mary?

5
One Heart, One Soul

Focus Point

////////////

You may remember from 50 years ago the play from existentialist thinker Jean-Paul Sartre called *"No Exit."* A line from that work became quite familiar and widespread, "Hell is others!" Many of us may have thought or felt how true that statement is, perhaps often. But our Christian experience and lived reality strongly contradict it. We, perhaps, might declare, "Hell is myself!" Yes, it is hell to be alone, isolated, without relationships, without social interaction, alone by myself. We human beings are meant to be with one another, to find our destiny and happiness with each other. Think of Jesus, "Love one another," which presupposes *"Be with* one another." The human community, especially the family, and the Christian community underscore the value of living in peace, non-competition, mutual respect, friendship and even love. It may be hard, and even painful to learn how to do this. After all, rubbing shoulders with others, to use a familiar idiom, may often feel like being polished with sandpaper. But there is no higher goal or happiness than this: brotherhood and sisterhood.

////////////

As for ourselves, we do not take any congregation for our model; we have no other model than the new-born Church. The Society began like the Church; we must be like the apostles and those who joined them and were already numerous. One heart and one soul. They loved each other like brothers. And then, ah!, no one knows what devotion the apostles had for the blessed Virgin! What tenderness for this divine mother! How they had recourse to her! Let us imitate them; let us see God in everything. (FS, 42, 3)

////////////

A family portrait

*C*olin often returns to this image of the origins: Mary surrounded by the apostles and several other disciples, forming one, congenial family group. Any one of us would certainly like to have been part of that group! Didn't people say of the first Christians, "Look how they love one another!"? In fact, in the Acts of the Apostles (2:41), Luke evokes the thousands of people who, as the Church comes into being, ask for baptism and to join the growing fellowship of the disciples. It is as if this fraternity, this mutual love were the *proof*, the witness to the Gospel message. Tying these events together may stretch the reality a little bit, but it does support what Colin tells us. Our attachment to Mary makes us brothers. Our fraternal union will be fertile, and our family will grow. And it will witness to the Gospel.

In reality, this brotherhood does not give evidence of any self-satisfaction of a group toward itself, brothers turned in on themselves, or an elite club for the initiated. It does happen that separate groups become individualized, each small unit becoming self-sufficient unto itself, not the least interested or concerned in what is happening to any other parallel group. But brotherhood has a double goal. On the one hand, it provides mutual interest and fraternal cooperation. And on the other, it is a call, an invitation to all those who want to become members. By its very nature, the brotherhood bears fruit both within and without the group.

So, when Colin recommends that the professors at the college in Belley, of which he is the superior, love one another as brothers, he also wants to inspire the students to do the same. And if he gives the same instructions to the missionaries leaving for Oceania, it's because spiritual and fraternal cooperation is pivotal to getting through the situations they will find themselves in.

Of course, when Colin sings the praises of that primordial unity he has his eyes fixed on the early Church, and also on the contemporary world that surrounds it. The union that he so ardently promotes stands in direct opposition to what he has seen in the Church and at all its levels of responsibility since his childhood: the attitude of "every man for himself" and how easily inequities are simply accepted and rationalized away. His way of reacting to these attitudes betrays his commitment to this ideal down to the tiniest details. Colin foresaw that all the priests, and not only the "coadjutor" or "auxiliary" brothers who serve them, should take their turn in the kitchen. And if the priests can drink coffee at the end of a meal, the brothers also have a right to it. Still more importantly, it goes without saying that the general chapter, that is, the full legislative assembly of the congregation, is not reserved only to authority figures, but to all religious, brothers as well as priests, whatever their work or responsibility. If a coadjutor brother is elected, he will take his seat in chapter. That is evident to everyone. We are not a society with a caste system; we are brothers.

Come back down to earth

"One heart, one soul." "To live as brothers." Let us admit at the start that our experience does not always match our highest desire to live the Christian life perfectly, as articulated so beautifully in these quotes. Perfection goes far beyond how well we conform to the law. The whole person is at stake in these formulas. Of course, we clearly understand that we are not talking about establishing amorous ties or friendships. After all, we always choose our own friends. But we do not choose our family members or our religious brothers; we simply accept and support them. "Support one another," St. Paul tells us (Col 3:13). And the noun *"supporter,"* used widely in the sports world for a fan who supports his team in the best of times and in the worst of times, conveys the message just as well as the verb. We try to be a *supporter* of our brothers just as much as we support them and they support us. And we know well the risks we can run when we try to live brotherhood, or family, or community, everywhere where we get down together for the same project. Anyone who dreams about some ideal community very much risks looking for it for a very long, long time, and by the same token he can cause a lot of damage to the community where he already lives.

There is, of course, no method for living together. Colin is not naïve about that. He is happy, rather, to give some practical points. He very much insists on mutual and affectionate respect. He speaks about "*civility*," delicacy, mutual consideration in language and appearance, as well as the occasions to "*honor*" our brothers. He insists on mutual forgiveness and encouragement and on regular renewal in the common life.

A fraternity available to everyone

In our time, the theme of fraternity is simply everywhere, at least in official texts. And it is always prominently inscribed on our public buildings.[a] More than ever, this is an idea which should be promoted.

First of all, it is a responsibility. In our world of extreme individualism that exalts the winner and his personal performance, fraternity gathers together and unites people. And when certain citizens are penalized by this or that physical, intellectual or social handicap, fraternity refuses to discriminate and takes care of all its members. And just as Colin recounts with an anecdote from his era, the traveler who is crossing through the forest in the dead of night

---

a. The reference here is to many public and government buildings in France bearing the carved motto over the main entrance: "Liberté, égalité, fraternité" (Freedom, Equality, Brotherhood) which was the motto of the French Revolution. [Translator's note]

is riddled with a thousand trepidations, real or imagined. But if he has a companion, they will talk to each other and the fears will vanish! Just so, fraternity is a path to walk together and to be safe together.

Secondly, fraternity is fertile. Of itself it produces fruit. It is attractive and welcoming. It practices hospitality, not only of the food and lodging type, which is already quite a bit. "If someone has anything against you, invite him to dinner" goes an old proverb, which certainly implies much more than setting out dishes in a food line. Hospitality from the heart requires much from the one being hospitable. And for those who receive it, it asks for nothing in return. It requires the fraternity to be genuinely available and flexible in its customs and attitudes so that a guest not only feels welcome but even expected.

Hospitality is the antidote for hostility, fear and distrust among people. It is also the open door to mutual discovery, and maybe even to mutual enrichment. A brotherhood which practices hospitality builds bridges.

There are so many expressions here that bring us gently back to our daily experiences in family, in community, at school, everywhere where we run into others. Let us not take them as challenges or disguised criticisms or even as regrets for all our failings in this area. But let us start, instead, with a prayer of thanksgiving for what each one has received from others, from family, or from friends and neighbors, from other Christians. "How good and how pleasant it is, when brothers dwell together as one!" (Ps 133:1).

Reflection Questions

If you grew up with brothers and sisters, did you experience rivalry and competition in your family? To what extent? Have you grown through it and out of it? If so, when did it happen and how did it happen? How would you describe love, loyalty, and compassion among your family members today? Have you experienced rivalry and competition in other areas: work, school, recreation, church, etc.? How do you feel about those experiences? Is it energizing? Distracting? How would you describe feelings of competition within yourself? Have you experienced an individual (even yourself) putting self before the group? What does that look like and feel like? What are the values of putting the group before self?

6
A Holy Cheerfulness

Focus Point

////////////

Thirty years ago the journalist, author and university professor Norman Cousins was diagnosed with a terminal disease, first thought to be cancer and then determined to be a rare and virulent form of arthritis. The prognosis was grim. But Cousins decided he would choose, no matter how hard it was, to have a positive attitude, to cultivate love and faith and hope, and above all to find as many reasons to laugh as he could. He had the full arsenal of Marx Brothers films, which he watched constantly. He charted the pain-killing effects of a belly laugh. He shared the laughter and the good humor with family, medical staff, everywhere he could. And he extended his life many years beyond his doctors' predictions. The power of a smile, the contagion of a hearty laugh. We understand these so well, at least in theory. But is it not so easy to feel cranky, to act crabby, to

70

show others how annoyed and frustrated we are? At its root, look how self-centered that behavior is. Poor me! So, are cheerfulness and spirituality related? Father Colin certainly knew that they are. He would easily have used a phrase from today, "Get over yourself!" Be cheerful and make others cheerful. Think of others and you will get way beyond your own insignificant little problems. You will get out of yourself and begin to taste happiness with others.

//////////////

How happy I am to see that the Marists have a certain breadth of virtue, a certain ease, full of abandonment. I encourage and establish this approach as far as I am able. When I say "I establish," I do not mean I talk about it, but I establish it by ways of doing things. At one time in a certain house they were rather stilted and strained, but now that has all changed. They are more magnanimous, they conduct themselves in a simple and happy fashion. Ah! If we did not always have a certain joy in our souls like this, a certain liberty, where would be the charm in our life? I do not like those who always have their hands joined, those whose devotion is narrow. (FS, 43)

//////////////

A different Colin?

"*Let yourselves be joyful; cheerfulness soothes nature.*" This is a surprising man. What he personally experienced in his life brought him to judge the world and the human race in a frankly negative, almost despondent way. And with this bleak and morose outlook, here is a man whom we might imagine as quite severe and difficult to be around, and now he appears in a completely different light! His contemporaries and his confreres call him cheerful, even when he is old and sick. They portray his way of acting as good, cheerful, fraternal. They note his "abandonment," his "casualness," as well as other attitudes of his that surprise us. Colin, the superior general, exalts the charm and merit of a "holy cheerfulness" in the community. He takes joy in it, while he criticizes narrow, fastidious devotion. Excessive rigor hurts everyone — both the one who practices it as well as those who witness it. We have to spread joy in others' hearts. "*Always be cheerful,*" he said to a confrere. A good religious is not necessarily the one who takes himself seriously and walks around in a perfectly prim way. This is always true and valid in all circumstances, but even more particularly when we educate young people. To require too much from them, to ask them to do too much, for too long a time, is to wear them out and discourage them.

Reminiscences from this time illustrate this character trait, especially when the early Marists describe, as they do often, what meals were like. Not that they were plentiful or elaborate, but especially because they lasted so long. The moment would come when the confreres would pull their chairs up to get close to Father Founder. During those extended times, he made everyone comfortable and "put their minds at ease." He was certainly a talented storyteller and artful raconteur with the knack of focusing on some comical detail in his stories. He would recall his innumerable adventures in the labyrinthine bureaucracy of Rome. And he astounded his confreres with that faculty he had that, in the midst of heavy and difficult matters, he could keep his detachment and the sense of humor about himself in all the situations he recounted, and he could communicate that to his listeners. At times like that, those at table said, "We laughed our hearts out; we were so happy; it was a real little feast" (FA, 386).

His whole life long Colin recalled the difficult beginnings of a little team of Marists in the overlooked villages of the Bugey mountain region. It would happen that hostile souls and troublemakers heckled the preachers during their sermons or threw rocks at them as they left town. Yet it seems that Colin could forget all that.

I particularly would like some memories of our first beginnings to remain in the Society. … Never were we so joyful; never did we laugh so heartily. I have always missed that time. (OM 2: 581, 1; 639, 1)

This is the same man who returns to his office and, with difficulty, has to deal with the latest situations in Oceania or endlessly has to find money to respond to the needs of the mission, notably the constant voyages to the Pacific, or has to respond to the needs of new implantations of the Society abroad or in the great cities at home. All this is in function of carrying on the work of spelling out and organizing the very life of his religious family.

You must spread joy in others' hearts

This message might strike us as a little puzzling. Does it really belong with our efforts to spiritually deepen our prayer? We are certainly well aware of the evils of our times which surround us, and we could even add to the list of woes. But we find it much more difficult to embrace the admonition, *"Always be cheerful."* Yet, generally speaking, no one would say that our church gatherings are famous for their joyfulness! Colin, in fact, invites us to look closely at what holds us back from being joyful. Thus, in his own way he tells us:

Stop that morbid contemplation of yourselves. Break out of the circle of your problems, your

disillusions and your fears. Open up the doors
and windows of your houses. Let in the fresh
air and the light of the Gospel.

He invites us to tear ourselves away from brooding over our problems and those of the Church. We often hear that ours is a Church "which, in any event, is now practically empty" and "where young people have stopped attending" and "where people wind up bored after all." He also asks us to tear ourselves away from obsessing over the list of our own failings, great or small, which we constantly resurrect and which tarnish the image that we have of ourselves and that we want to project to others. We could well take up as our own Colin's urgent appeal:

Let us not always be coming back upon our-
selves, let us not look at ourselves so much.
Really, what a spectacle! "We are so fine!"
Rather, let us look to God, who is uncreated
beauty. (EK 546)

As he said this, he laughed heartily. "Ah yes,"
he said, "we soil ourselves with our own com-
pany." (FS 54, 3)

A message always good to listen to

We can see in Colin's dealings with life a certain way of staying detached from whatever happened to him and from whatever others did to him. And by the same token, he had that way of reclaiming the true meaning of this event or that statement. We would do well not to pass over too quickly what appears only as a pleasant or curious occurrence. Jesus himself tells us something in that regard (Mk 2:19). The wedding guests are not going to fast as long as the bridegroom is with them. So, when Jesus is in our midst, it is better to take advantage of his presence and rejoice in it rather than brood over our sins.

Let's not move too quickly to shelve humor away in a cupboard. The word "humor" has the same root as "humility." After all, to take the drama out of situations, as Colin does, is to recover the real value of people and things. It means to give space for hope. Holy cheerfulness, pure joy, is something like shades of color in the weather: a ray of brilliant sunshine on a gray day; a sun's ray that does not blot out things that are not so attractive, but actually lets us see them in a new light.

Without at all forgetting our concerns, let us thank the Lord for all that brings us happiness and joy in creation, joy in our relationships or in our work or in our projects. Let us thank him for what is good and beautiful in our lives and in the lives of those we love. And finally, let us make our own this advice from Colin:

> *Let us laugh, since God wants us to laugh.*
> *We can weep some other time.*

And let us borrow from Mary her thanksgiving song: "I rejoice in God my Savior."

Reflection Questions

It is a sad fact these days that many people suffer from anxiety, sometimes not too deeply and sometimes so deeply that it requires medical or professional attention. Given that reality and after reflecting on Day 6, are you attracted to the idea of Holy Cheerfulness? Have you experienced it personally or seen it in others? How do you see yourself growing in cheerfulness? Is it easier to be cheerful in the presence of others rather than by yourself? How does that work? Have you ever cheered up someone else? How did that happen? Could you do it again? How do you feel when you do it? For you, how does Holy Cheerfulness fit within the Gospel message? Within the Marist ideal?

7
Like Mary

Focus Point

////////////

In Day 7, we touch on two truly transcendent realities, which means that we may need some help to understand them. The first is the phrase "gracious choice." Perhaps "gratuitous" choice would explain it better. Mary has chosen, says Fr. Colin. She has chosen individuals to be in her family and, thus, bear her name. But her choice is free, not predicated on some prior condition, not earned, not deserved, totally free. The parallel is God's grace. In fact, from the word "grace" we derive "gracious." I cannot earn God's grace or love; it simply flows overabundantly without my deserving it, paying for it, or bargaining for it. We understand very well the theory, but we frequently forget it or overlook it in our approach to God or Mary. The second item is Fr. Colin's unique insight into a Marist's relationship with Mary. Centuries of Christian spirituality have offered the holy practice of "imitation." It says that we grow in holiness and virtue, like humility or patience or good temper, by imitating Jesus or Mary, or some other saint. Take a particular virtue and try to practice it in our lives the way Mary practiced it, but now in our everyday life with acts of the same particular virtue. Methodical people would even take a new virtue each month, trying to make as much progress as possible. It certainly is a good method for spiritual growth. But on the other hand, Fr. Colin's perception teaches us that a Marist has been chosen, freely, to be a member of Mary's family. Hence, the Marist is already "identified" with Mary. A Marist is an extension of Mary in the world. As a child will resemble (identify with) its mother in physical features, and usually in some actions, perhaps in the way she laughs, or prepares tea, or greets a friend. With or without imitation, a Marist will already have the face of Mary, the voice of Mary, the heart of Mary in our world today. Marists "think, judge, feel and act as Mary." (SM Priests' Constitutions)

//////////////

Let them [Marists] always bear in mind that they belong by a gracious choice to the family of the blessed Mary, Mother of God, from whose name they are called Marists, and whom they have chosen from the beginning as their model and their first and perpetual superior. If therefore they are and desire to be true sons of this dear Mother, let them try constantly to breathe her spirit: a spirit of humility, self-denial, intimate union with God, and the most ardent love of neighbor. So they must think as Mary, judge as Mary, feel and act as Mary in all things, otherwise they will be unworthy and degenerate son. (C 228)

///////////////

A profound conviction

" *L**ike Mary." "In Mary's way."* These expressions often flow from Colin's pen. Mary, he writes, is the first and perpetual superior of her religious family. He constantly invites and encourages Marists to do nothing, to say nothing, to undertake nothing without looking to her, bringing to her all their questions, their plans, their actions:

> *Holy Mother, what should I say? What should I do?*

And of course, they should act like her: discreetly, quietly, and without commotion. Toward the end of his life, Colin revealed this unusual secret which confirms his attachment to Mary:

> *O good Mother, the Society is your work. If only I had been a mere passive instrument, it would all have gone much better; it is because I mixed in something of my own that we have these misfortunes.* (EK 167)

Nothing at all of that tenor shows up in his personal devotion, prayer or worship. The same goes for his spiritual and theological writings on Mary. Colin is interested, first of all, in making Mary's behavior his own, that is, the actions of the mother and the disciple of Jesus as the Scriptures describe her to us — but there is so little there! Hers is a behavior that brings together in a paradoxical way a strong, real presence, a determined commitment when it is called for, like the annunciation, Cana, the crucifixion, together with an almost absolute discretion, marked by few words, the absence of show or dramatic declarations, but rather listening and pondering the events.

Look for the woman

Colin's project is meant to be taken up in each generation. Here in our twenty-first century, how can we find a way of being and living in conformity with what is Mary's unique life? Colin helps us answer this by sending us back to the Scriptures, suggesting that we look to Nazareth, Cana, and several other episodes in the public life of Jesus as recorded in the Gospel, the death of Jesus and, of course, the Resurrection and what takes place afterwards.

Mary, in the sequence of women in the Bible, enabled the plan of salvation that God was pleased to decree in Christ to become reality with the "Yes" she gave the angel. This is what she expresses in her *Magnificat*, taking up words, phrases, prayers uttered by all the women who preceded her and who collaborated in their own ways to fulfill God's salvific design for the world. Later, she would help Jesus to take the decisive step toward his mission and would urge him to launch his public life. At that point he seemed to hesitate, "My hour has not yet come." She then said to him at Cana, perhaps to provoke a little, "They have no more wine," and to the servants she said, "Do whatever he tells you." She, too, is tuned to her son's word, and it increases her confidence in him all the more when she hears his teaching that the bonds of blood relationship are not at all the most significant, but that "the one who hears the word of God and keeps it" has value in his eyes. As a result, she undergoes the transition from mother to disciple.

Take another Scripture scene. She experienced this one like a second annunciation, or a second childbirth, and this one so much more intensely painful. As her son is dying, he commends his disciple to her. "Woman, behold your son." From that moment the disciple took her into his home. And here we have the mother of the first Christian community, the mother of the Church!

Mary and us, Mary and me

Having a wonderful relationship with Mary is not automatic! She sometimes may appear distant, a statue hidden behind obscure invocations from the litany: "Tower of David," "Seat of Wisdom," "Queen of Angels." Here is a woman with an exceptional destiny, so far distant from our own, the Mother of Jesus and the Mother of God, immaculate Virgin, completely sinless and now already raised and assumed into heaven. And yet, she has so much that she still wants to share with us.

An interior woman. When everything in our world draws us toward the things we have to do, the decisions we have to make, when we have to yield to others' requests, when we are besieged by facts and data from the whole world, then we remember — she pondered all these things in her heart.

She was a mother at Bethlehem and a mother on Calvary. She comes from Nazareth with the son who grew up next to her, the same son who later traversed the roads of Palestine. And even if she does not always understand him, she puts her trust in him and lets him accomplish "his mission."

Here is a woman who is concerned about her son. Having gone through the forty-day preparation, he nevertheless continued to attract opposition and contradiction of all kinds. If someone had told his mother, "He is of age, he's an adult," she would have answered, "Yes, but I am always his mother."

When the evil one suggests that we just stop trying, hinting: "What's the use?", Mary points to her son and says, "Do whatever he tells you." And even when she might have had reasons to abandon hope, the Scripture portrays her standing there where her son is dying. To bear her name, to choose her as our model, does not mean to repeat the Gospel word for word, but rather to give Mary space in our lives so that she can act as she did with Jesus, that she can be the bearer of hope, and so that she can share her trust in life and her faith in her son's word.

We could each ask the question: What does it mean to welcome the word of God just as Mary did in her daily life at Nazareth? What does it mean to treasure all these things and ponder them in our heart? How can we interpret this expression as an invitation to move into our interior self, not as backing out of life, but as a retreat, as detaching ourselves so as to plumb the depth of things, of words or of events? How do we learn to welcome whatever comes our way, especially the unexpected and the difficult?

How can Mary, a woman on the journey, accompany us in the different journeys we have to accomplish in our lives? These journeys are sometimes quite simple and natural, but not any easier for that — the journey of aging, the journey of health toward debility, the journey of activity to inactivity or from inactivity to commitment, my faith journey ("I don't believe anymore what I used to"), journeys in my relations with others, between parents and children or grandchildren, the occasional painful journeys in the changes my Church community has undergone, and so many others. And even more, Mary can help us *to be* journeys for others — a bridge or even a bearer of others.

Mary is the woman who wants to live and bring others to life. She chooses life!

Mary is present at all of life's choices!

Mary is always interested in whoever comes to life, always interested in life!

Reflection Questions

In today's reflection on Mary, and with your knowledge of Mary in the Scriptures and in Catholic devotion, please name the characteristics or traits of Mary that speak the most strongly to you. Are you attracted to having those same traits yourself? How do you understand imitating a virtue that you find in Jesus or in Mary? If you grow more *like* them, do you think you grow *closer to* them? How does that work? What does it feel like to actually be a member of Mary's family, being her beloved son or daughter, and therefore bearing her very name? What emotions does that stir up within you — Gratitude? Enthusiasm? Love for others? Compassion? Any others?

8
Say "No"

Focus Point

////////////////////

In the reflections for Day 8, we come to a reality and insight from Fr. Colin that may be somewhat out of our range to grasp. This is not for lack of knowledge or wisdom, but from a lack of perspective. When you are too close to something, it is sometimes impossible to see. We are being invited to be self-critical and critical of our culture. How objective can we be about values we live every day and breathe almost like air? Can we be objective about the degree to which we are caught up in consumerism? Are we free in our decisions about the various goods we need or want? To what extent does someone else (e.g., advertising) tell me what to do? Father Colin, of course, does not say a word about advertising, but he does challenge us to be free in all our choices, especially to be free to say "no" when it's appropriate. Earlier generations might have labeled this way of choosing as self-discipline, self-control, or even sacrifice. Whatever you call it, it is a perfect practice for our times, because it leads us directly to freedom. Also in Day 8, we return to the concept of God's gratuity or gratuitousness, his "graciousness," in that God's love, friendship, forgiveness, etc. are always unmerited, undeserved, and unearned. God is Freedom, and, as a result, he acts and gives freely.

//////////////

Let them hold all covetousness in horror. Yes, indeed, may we abhor this spirit. I have seen in the rules of certain congregations that they should strive to win over people in high places, to curry favor with them.... Personally, I have taken the opposite course, and I say that confidence placed in a creature, whoever it may be, is always to the detriment of the creator. It is so much detraction from the good Lord. Speaking for myself, when I have some plan in mind and the thought comes to me, "Such and such a person could be of use to you," I dismiss it immediately, and I say in defiance of myself, "Yes, and then the blessed Virgin will leave you to fend for yourself," when she sees that you are looking elsewhere for your resources. (FS 54, 2)

//////////////

To hell with cupidity!

*T*he word "cupidity" is charged with meaning for Colin, and he veers away from it. Merely to evoke the concept of greed plunges him into a fury. It provokes a real psychological repugnance in him. He shows the same aversion for pride and for the desire for power, and he pitches them into the same trash bin with cupidity. This antipathy does not at all contradict his fidelity to the Church. What he denounces is behavior that directly clashes with the Gospel, the very Gospel that clerics are supposed to proclaim! All this goes against Mary's spirit. How explain this particular target of his and the vehemence? We have to go back to a most unfortunate experience in his childhood and how he analyzed the type of society he was living in.

This childhood experience could be a scene taken right out of the Marx Brothers! He had just entered his teen-age years, when Jean-Claude Colin fell gravely ill. Everyone thought he was going to die. His family had gathered around his bed, convinced that he had fallen unconscious. He could hear, however, everything they were saying and especially their conversation about what kind of inheritance he would leave behind and how they would divide it up. He had been an orphan for a long time, and supposedly his parents had left him a fortune. The way his family behaved revolted him.

More deeply, this event brought him to ana-
lyze the situation of France in general at that
time, and of the Church in particular. His attitude is quite lucid toward a part of the upper
clergy, their wealth and how their personal concerns prevail over any sense of pastoral care. He
saw the damage caused by the distances between
the upper and the lower clergy, the mutual distrust, the misunderstandings that led inevitably
to the falling away of the laity. He noted that
the Jesuits, whom he otherwise greatly admired,
have paid dearly for their relationships, their net-
works of influence among the powerful of this
world. All that carrying on earned for them a
severe backlash — the pope dissolved the congregation, and they were expelled from France,
resulting in heaps of scorn upon them.

Colin's contempt for greed is relentless. We
find it again in the Constitutions he wrote for
the Marist Fathers, evoking the radical opposition "between the spirit of Mary and the spirit of
ambition, covetousness, and the lust for power"
(C 92). The Gospel translates this even more
clearly with Jesus' teaching, "No one can serve
two masters."

Always more

It is simply self-evident to make comparisons
with our world as we know it. Greed and cupidity, as Colin denounces them, seem so very

much the "always more" or "never enough" syndrome of our times. To succeed you have to be a performer, a winner. And to do that, it is good "to have connections" and to give in to the demands of the time or of fashion, to be "socially correct." To put it briefly, you have to go "with the times."

Before we denounce society completely, let's take a look in the mirror. Surely we will not recognize someone crazed with greed, or ravenous for power and money, or an interloper among the great and near-great! But let's take our cue from Colin and ask ourselves: Does it ever happen that we find our "image" at risk if we dare to offer a "no" which might displease others — "no" to plans, or behaviors, or situations that we judge unacceptable, based on our faith or quite simply on our respect for others? Or do we prefer to conform because we do not want to risk our good reputation? And so we act "as if," or rather we make pretense of seeing nothing and hearing nothing.

To make progress in my life — my family life, religious life, professional life — what are the "no's" I have to utter? What holds me back from saying them? We are not talking here about being a curmudgeon or a prude, but we are rather considering the great service we can offer the community and ourselves by thus pronouncing a "no," not for the pleasure of forbidding something, but saying the "no" that can give structure and that can even make us a little more free.

Arrogance, complacency, attachment to money are all things that can threaten me. I can fall into the trap under the best pretexts. I want to "do well" in my involvement in the parish, in my family, in my religious community. The danger is not so much to "succeed" as to think of myself as the master of my success, depriving God of his part! Unfortunately, we all know examples of human successes which have virtually devoured their victims, the people who become closed in on themselves, those who attribute all their success to themselves, withdrawn from others and so satisfied with their work, an entire human life focused on and trapped by their own human plans while they turn all attention away from God!

And then there are the daily events we are so used to: repeated disloyalties, the endless routine of work, how weary the days grow, concern for our reputation, and so many other worries.

For the honor of God

Why is there a need to set up road signs, "*Caution*," "*Danger*"? Because, for Colin, what is at stake here is the honor of God.

God is not on the side of cupidity; he is on the side of generosity. But we find that difficult to grasp. We multiply whatever we think we have to do for our salvation and the salvation of the world. And God tells us that he will save us by love and generosity. We insist that God give us gifts that we think we need. And he tells us, "But you already have your hands full — of your own plans, your projects, your methods, and your words. Your hands are so full that I can no longer slip in even the tiniest thing."

We are naturally proud to present our work to God. "See what I have done!" And we hardly hear him tell us, "Do not forget that it is, first of all, my work, and that I have chosen you to be my instrument. You are not on your own here."

We think that it is important for us to "do" something, to produce something. And yet God asks us, from time to time, to simply take the time to be, to exist, before him, and to do so peacefully, graciously, without an apparent outcome, and, as bizarre as it might seem, to let ourselves be loved. Let us turn over to him our desire, our good will, our talents, as well as our awkwardness and our infidelity. When the right time comes, he will know how to turn us into the workers that he needs.

In our prayer let us give the last word to graciousness. And let us linger as long as we need to on Mary's words, "The Lord has filled the hungry with good things, and the rich he has sent away empty."

Reflection Questions

In Day 8 we have reflected on the historical origins of Fr. Colin's vehement condemna-
tion of (a) greed, (b) the desire for attention or
acclaim, and (c) a thirst for power, especially
the power that wants to lord itself over others.
We also heard the challenge to look at ourselves
in the mirror first before judging others. Do you
detect any of those flaws within yourself? Do
you see how seductive they can be? Trying to
be both objective and charitable, do you see any
of those flaws in our Church today, in church
leadership? Do you see how those vices can
turn people away from the Gospel? Can you
think of any practical and effective antidotes to
these pervasive flaws? For yourself first of all,
what would they be? Secondly, for others? No
one can make another person change, but can
you imagine good antidotes that others, like
church leaders, might adopt?

9
Unknown and, *as it Were,* Hidden in the World

Focus Point

//////////////

The reflection for today, Day 9, brings us to one of the most beautiful, yet one of he subtlest facets of the Marist charism, "hidden and unknown." While it lies deep within the mystery of the charism, it is not, in fact, the goal or aim of the Society of Mary. If it were, then everything Marists did would have to lead directly to achieving that goal. Marists would be evaluated for how hidden and how unknown they were. The goal of Marists, however, is to do Mary's work, what she wants done – namely, reconciling her children with her Son, converting sinners, and bringing the Gospel message to all the world. In evaluating how well Marists accomplish those goals, we use an auxiliary measure, "How hidden and unknown were they when they were working toward the goal?" What we are dealing with here is doing our best, doing everything we can, to achieve our goal, but not to make a show, not seek attention or notoriety, rather to give all that up. As we reflected in Day 8, this requires self-discipline, self-control, even sacrifice. This also means putting all the attention and interest on the other person, the one who wants to meet Jesus. Day 9 also brings us into an extremely interesting reflection on God as hidden. At various times in history, even recently, God was pronounced dead! While not accepting that declaration or the statement that God is absent, we would certainly acknowledge that for many people God has gone into hiding. But aren't there some advantages to that? Isn't a hidden God far less fierce and terrifying than a bombastic judge and punisher? Doesn't a hidden God let us free, without his compulsion, to come to our own conclusions? And does it not also let God be free to court and woo us, to urge us to fall in love with him freely, because we want to?

///////////////

Father Colin was speaking of the hidden life which should be the life of the Society, and he said: That, Gentlemen, is one of the characteristics of the Society, the one by which it should be distinguished, in accordance with the particular spirit of its vocation, from the others which have preceded it, which others I neither judge nor condemn. The animosity

*which some of them encounter does not all stem, it
seems to me, from hatred for religion. In several cases,
the alienation could also come in part from the style
these communities have adopted.... Let us try to adopt
a modest way of behaving, one which gives the least
possible offense to those among whom we live and
which is in conformity with our vocation and the spirit
of the blessed Virgin whose name we bear.* (FS 146, 4)

//////////////

The origin of an expression

*T*he first Marists report that the expression *"hidden and unknown"* came up frequently in Colin's ideas and talks. *"The whole
spirit of the Society is there,"* he used to say. What
we know for sure is that this phrase has been
handed down to all generations of Marists from
the beginning, something like a password. At
times, the interpretation seems tentative. Is it
an invitation to humility, or to restraint, or to
avoid pushing oneself forward? It might also be
the fruit of Colin's reflection on what his times
were like. He certainly reflects on what he sees
and experiences, particularly the setbacks of the
Society of Jesus which had been suppressed by
the pope between 1773 and 1814. The Jesuits
paid dearly for their prominence. Colin com-
mented, *"We must not attract attention to ourselves.
We must not provoke it"* (FS 89, 6).

But we have to dig deeper to find the sense of this expression, *"It was addressed to a soul."* He would say that phrase and mean, of course, "Mary addressed it." Once again, the original setting of Mary and the apostles inspired Colin and guided his experience. This is the attitude that Mary had at the beginning of the Church.

> *Did she create a stir? The Gospel says very little about her, very little, yet it was she who drew down graces from heaven upon the earth.* (EK 356)

Mary understands that nothing can be forced or imposed. Her motherly attitude of encouraging, watching over and exercising patience helped the Church come to birth and grow. Doesn't God himself act like this? Already the story of Elijah teaches us that God reveals himself far better in a tiny breath wrapped within a silent stillness rather than in a thunder blast.

The formula that Colin spent his whole life deepening turns out to be a wise response to a particular pastoral situation of his time. The common people remembered the burdens the Church imposed upon them, certain taxes they had to pay, and the pastor's authority which he did not hesitate to exert to regulate their personal or family lives. The French Revolution and the succeeding Napoleonic Empire both contributed to spreading ideas from the Enlightenment — freedom of thought, reason in opposition to faith, and the freedom to choose one's opinions in any area whatsoever. Hence, *"We must not attract attention to ourselves." "We must not provoke it"* (FS 89, 6). We have to abandon anything which, whether in small or in great degree, could smack of a desire to impose the faith on another or which looks like the slightest form of triumphalism. We are not on mission for our benefit. We are first of all and only on mission to serve the proclamation of the Gospel. And we have to cultivate enough confidence to let the Truth speak for itself. It will come across quite well on its own authority.

Can we adopt this formula as our own?

Colin invites us to pursue this pastoral reflection for our own times. Is the formula *"hidden and unknown"* still relevant today? Would the time ever come to proclaim the Good News with trumpet blasts or with bombastic and triumphant oratory?

Certainly, the Church no longer lords it over the people as it did in the nineteenth century. In our day, she is rather of no consequence to people and even seems quaint. Her rhetoric appears too defensive, or inappropriate, or beside the point. People think today that the Church is taken up with things that do not concern her, and that it would be better if she minded her own business. And it has been quite a long time now that people simply move away from and leave the Church without suffering any adverse consequences. Then there has recently been so much commotion and publicity about the Church, it is probably a much better thing not to be allied with it. So how can we translate this expression *"hidden and unknown"* for our contemporaries in a way that still suggests a real and concrete presence?

The words themselves already lead us to a preliminary statement. If Marists want to be present to the world, they refuse to call attention to themselves. They prefer a presence which is discreet, entirely directed toward others. Neither are they very interested in what people say about them or think about them. And above all, this attention that they pay to the other person presupposes a patient and active listening to what it is that brings the person life, that hurts him, that gives him hope, and perhaps even what his deepest fears are.

So, I take the time to welcome another person just as he presents himself, without judgment or rejection, and I acknowledge him in his uniqueness, without trying to put him in a manageable category or stick a label on him. And maybe a simple gesture, a word, or even a lovely silence that comes from my heart will be able to touch his heart. And little by little you begin to realize that the encounter itself has become the message, when two people face each other in a humble sharing of their life and hope. We can certainly call all that "unknown and hidden," but what it means essentially is getting close to the other person, sharing that we are just as vulnerable as he is, just as subject to doubts as she is. And I am free to speak of myself, of what is going on within me and where I draw my joy in living.

Colin's time and our times today have something in common, the difficult relationship with the Church and with God! In both cases, but for different reasons and in different ways, it is God who stays hidden and unknown. And this is often because of the very people who are entrusted with making him known. How true it was in Colin's time that the Church, the clergy, the lifestyles and ways of communicating deterred people rather than speaking to them of God. As for today, everywhere we hear the rallying cries for Jesus! the Gospel! Evangelical movements! But, is there anything about the Church? No. As if the Church were some kind of stumbling block to the message of Christ.

In this kind of atmosphere, all our words are booby-trapped, and dogmatic declarations will not necessarily help people to understand. What we have left are attitudes, gestures, and acts of listening so extremely well, that these will help us to recognize, despite whatever awkward words there might be, a desire, even a restlessness, and a wish to take a step toward the spiritual! God, who is himself hidden and unknown, brings himself to the encounter. And here we can again recall Colin. This is not the time to be dogmatic or to talk about ourselves, but rather to share with others, like a secret, something that speaks to us of God.

These encounters are not reserved to priests or to religious. We could ask ourselves, therefore, what our attitudes, our intentions, and our lifestyle can say (or not say) about God around us. We could recall the Gospel passages where Jesus said he would be present, when we visited the sick or those in prison, when we shared our food with the hungry and poor, with strangers. And we should certainly ask ourselves whether this attitude of *"hidden and unknown"* has prepared us, in long stretches of silence and patience and in deep prayer, to welcome God *"unknown and as it were hidden."*

Reflection Questions

We occasionally hear of the "hidden life of Jesus," his 30 years in Nazareth preparing for his public ministry. Although we know absolutely nothing about that period, can you imagine what it might have been like in the home of Jesus, Mary and Joseph? From a spiritual angle, what are the advantages of anonymity?

We are familiar with the parable of the Good Samaritan and how highly Jesus praised him. Is it possible to be an *anonymous* Good Samaritan? What would one be like? What would it take for you to be "hidden and unknown" in your relations with others, in your daily life, etc.? Would it be easy, hard, etc.? What would be the advantages for you to try such an approach?

10

Salvation before the Law

Focus Point

////////////

In today's reflection we come face to face with the God of Mercy and Jesus the Compassionate One. Father Colin had the inspired insight that Marists were always to be "instruments of divine Mercy." What a beautiful call as well as a challenge. Although our culture and religious practices have obviously changed vastly in these last 200 years, Mercy still lies at the heart of a Marist's ministry. Let us try to imagine the context of Fr. Colin's times. Naturally, he was thinking as a priest, one of whose central ministries was to hear confessions, forgive and reconcile sinners, to extend God's mercy in the confessional, and "to save souls." That is surely a phrase we do not use today, but in those times it included the deepest concern for the salvation of others, and with that a real love for others. Father Colin realized the

incomprehensible gift he had to share with sinners by giving absolution. He would use any law,
he said, or any rule, or any loophole to absolve
a penitent. He recognized the huge advantage he
and the other itinerant missionaries enjoyed as
they stayed in a village for a short two or three
weeks. Villagers could come to confess truly
anonymously and never have to worry about seeing these priests again. For example, many fami-
lies lived in what had been the parish rectory, the
priest's house, which they had purchased from the
civil authorities. In some instances, after the res-
toration of the Church in France, some of those
very priests returned to their former villages.
Father Colin wondered how could the new occu-
pants (of perhaps ten years or more) ever confess
their sins to this local priest, risking his wrath and
the possible punishment of being evicted from
houses where they had lived for years. A Marist
will always think first about the salvation of a sinner.

//////////////

*How I long for this notion of mercy to take root
in all our men! Oh! How much easier it is to get rid
of dangerous elements than to convert them. It is not
zeal to send away straight off what stands in the way
of good. If so, the matter would be quickly settled.
Our Lord did not take that line. Such would not be
the spirit of God. We must do all we can, try every*

means, pray, and it is only as a last resort that we lop off the branch.

Personally, I pardon two, three times, and I am not afraid of doing this, because I say to the good Lord, "My God, this is the way you act." (FA 206, 9–10)

///////////////

A providential meeting

*I*t did not take Colin, a practical man full of good sense, a long time to discover that the pastoral approach to the Sacrament of Penance in force during his ministry could not really reach the people he came into contact with every day. As a priest he was meeting men, women, and young people "in the field" who had just come out of a most painful fifteen or twenty years of serious hardships. Every one of them had been touched, whether near or far, by the attempt to destroy Christianity and erode any sense of public morality. One practical issue many people faced was how could they return as full members of the Christian community after they had willingly acquired various Church goods and property which had been confiscated by the Revolution and then been declared public goods and property and sold to ordinary people? Another problem was how could they face others in good faith if they had taken advantage of the Revolution's anti-Church law permitting divorce? And then in Colin's times, there was the whole issue of settling scores among villagers regarding the pastor or assisting priests in the local parishes — had they taken the oath of allegiance to the Revolutionary Constitution, thus separating themselves from the Church, or had they refused to swear the oath? Still more deeply felt was the disruption everywhere in daily life after the collapse of all the structures of the "*Ancien Régime*."[a] Now where were they headed?

Moving from theory to practice

When the Marists began their pastoral ministry, they were between twenty-five and thirty years of age. Colin understood very quickly that they could not approach the people about confession in the old style, with endless discussions about the gravity of their sins and a sacramental encounter that resembled a judicial tribunal, with embarrassing inquiries, impossible penances, and absolutions programmed over the space of several months. The God of that type of confession is a formidable God, terrifying to the sinner, and he has nothing to do with the father of the prodigal son.

---

a. "Earlier Order," a term referring to the ensemble of monarchy, aristocracy, government, church and society which functioned in the centuries before the French Revolution (1789-1799). One of the aims of the Revolution was to abolish the "*Ancien Régime.*" [Translator's note]

It turns out that Colin, who was by nature rather timorous and scrupulous, had the immense good fortune to have as his bishop in Belley, Alphonse Devie, a disciple of the great Italian moral theologian St. Alphonsus de Liguori, the founder of the Redemptorists. During most of his life, this great saint fought to put things back in their rightful place, to place the penitent back at the heart of the confession, to get rid of anything that smacks of rigorism or fear, and thus to make the penitent the beneficiary of a special sacramental moment filled with God's love rather than an emphasis on justice or the fear of God.

Colin seized this opportunity and pursued all the consequences of that pastoral attitude supported by his own bishop. Finished now would be the terrifying fire-and-brimstone sermons in the rural missions, during which the preacher dwelt on the torments of sinners in hell. No longer would the priests go to the homes of reluctant parishioners and force them to come to the services! For the people already frightened by what had happened to them, particularly for the youngest, it was much more effective to show a friendly face which would say something about that mercy which they were certainly looking for.

What if Colin came back today?

Of course, our present situation is not the same. Our contemporaries are not generally very concerned about going back to a Christian culture, which they never knew in the first place, and which seems to them washed up and obsolete. Would there be any doubt about that?

Liguori's moral principles are certainly not of his own invention. If they appealed to some of the clergy at Colin's time, it is because they put the spotlight back on the Gospel message buried so long especially under the hairsplitting quibbles of Jansenism, which claimed that God has reserved his grace for his privileged favorites. The theme of mercy is at the heart of Scripture, at the heart of God's self-revelation. Yahweh loves his children infinitely beyond their sins. Jesus interpreted this message when he declared that he had come not to save the just but to save sinners. And he chose, to the great displeasure of "the just," to be openly on the side of disreputable men and women.

Are our contemporaries, that is, family members, friends, and neighbors, far from these issues? Confession and sin? Perhaps. Nevertheless, wouldn't "mercy" mean something to them? In the Latin root for our word "mercy" (*misericordia*), we see something of "misery" and something of "heart." When others are suffering misery, it is mercy that goes out to them. And everyone shares in some kind of misery or other, and everyone knows what "heart" is. Anyone among us, no matter who, could be that person who, behind the façade, struggles with personal, emotional and professional problems and who, as a result, bears a heavy burden. And today's young people are themselves familiar with a kind of distress, which is different from their nineteenth-century ancestors, but which is just as oppressive.

Colin's reflection and his way of acting send us back to examine our own attitudes. Let us try to hold off on our judgments about "the world," about others, and about the young. To this point, Colin wrote:

> *You have to offer young people a helping hand, go along with what is needed and not be too demanding. I take a broad path, I wait till their faith grows.* (FS 40, 4)

He "takes a broad path," that is, he accepts their limits. It is so much easier to dismiss someone than to try to understand! Don't we hear people sometimes tell us that the Church is not welcoming, that she is even intolerant? Before we go all out to show our complete agreement with them, we could well ask ourselves about how we welcome people and what is our threshold for tolerance! We have to "offer a helping hand," as Colin says.

As the sacrament of Reconciliation unfolds, there is the opening sentence that almost everyone says, "Bless me, Father, for I have sinned." Can you catch something incongruous here?

"Bless" means to say something good, to wish someone well, to hope the best for someone. And the request here is based on the fact that the person has sinned. It would be more logical to say, "Do not bless me, Father, because I have sinned, and I am not worthy to be blessed." And, yet, we mean and understand the opposite, which then requires us to reflect on the approach we are taking. The miracle here is that God's mercy lets us make this approach and that this approach is more valuable in gaining us his grace, and his grace is yet another proof of his love.

Our contemporaries are most often distant from the Church. To recall for them the Church's norms, or practices, or moral positions will have practically no effect on them, except unfortunately to revive some awful memories. But a face-to-face encounter which displays confidence and a sense of "I was waiting for you" or "I was hoping you would come," along with "You can tell me anything you want," will produce a much better result. It is up to each one of us to find the right words and gestures to help the other person hear within himself a voice telling him, "You are worth much more than what you do. I am not interested in your sins. I am interested in you and your coming back to me, today."

Reflection Questions

Since much of today's reflection focused on the Sacrament of Reconciliation, can you describe some of your best experiences in Confession? Some of your worst? What makes the difference? Outside the realm of church or religion, please describe occurrences of great mercy or compassion that you've seen. If you've seen the opposite, namely cruelty or contempt, can you describe that? Some cultures believe that extending mercy, and especially forgiveness, betrays a person's weakness. How would you respond to this?

11
Mary at the Beginning, Mary at the End

Focus Point

////////////

The precious legacy of Christianity is hope. Jesus' parting words, "Behold, I am with you all days, even unto the end of the world," and his promise, "I will send you the Spirit, the Comforter, who will teach you and guide you until I return," should inspire us with the deepest trust and confidence. Now in Day 11, the Marist narrative presents Mary solemnly declaring, "I was the support of the Church at her birth, and I will be so in the last days." Ever since Jesus uttered those words, can we say that the world has gotten better, at least from a spiritual point of view? Of course, there is no doubt about that. But at the same time, our age has seen an explosion of evil and depravity without precedent. A truly Christian and Marist response is not to capitulate or despair, but to trust deeply in Jesus and also in Mary. As Marists, we are called to confront the world, engage our present times. We are challenged to value what we find as good and sincere and to try to bring back to Jesus whoever has gone astray. After all, our age, indeed every age, are the "last days."

///////////////

Gentlemen, [here his tone became solemn], I do not mind repeating it here once more: the words "I was the mainstay of the new-born Church; I shall be again at the end of time," served us, in the very earliest days of the Society, as a foundation and an encouragement. They were always before us. We worked in that direction, so to speak. We must admit that we are living in very bad times; humanity is really sick. At the end of time it will need a great deal of help, and the blessed Virgin will be the one to give it. Gentlemen, let us rejoice to belong to her Society and bear her name. The other communities being established [at this time] envy us our fine name. (FS 152, 10)

///////////////

The times are bad

*C*olin was convinced of this — the blessed Virgin, present at the birth of the Church will be just as present at the end of time. This presence of Mary fostered the Church's first steps. We find it again now, thought Colin, and it will produce the same effects. Furthermore, the age in which Colin himself lived he saw as quite close to the end times, and those times were quite evil. He was categorical on this point, and he never ran out of words to describe his century, the nineteenth: indifference, disbelief, ignorance, materialism, and paganism. *"Poor reason! It is ruining the world."* And philosophy *"is paving the way for the end of time"* (EK 100). The Enlightenment and the French Revolution had definitely left their stamp!

Thus, more than ever, we have to count on Mary's presence and support to help us confront dangers. Toward this end, in that century which Mary, he thought, wanted to create this religious family bearing her name, not to exercise this or that particular ministry or to promote a specific Marian devotion, but to bring to birth, to bring to *rebirth* the Church in this unique and specific moment. And here's a first point we may find astounding. Colin developed a deeply pessimistic view of the world, but far from discouraging him, it actually invited him to think of a new Church, a new proclamation of the Gospel!

The times are still bad

No one is forced to apply Colin's judgments on his "age" as necessarily literal for our day. But let us agree that his vocabulary, although obviously dated, does correspond quite well to our times. And we might consider that what was only in germ at Colin's time has undergone a wide development ever since.

This is not the place to propose a detailed analysis of all the mutations in contemporary society. But there are many aspects of our age that we may find troubling and disconcerting. And then those occasions happen to us that leave us simply confused and sometimes conflicted, like the gradual disappearance of all prohibitions or the frequent challenges to all levels of authority. We have experienced how society exalts the individual, his right to happiness and to a freedom which has the first and last word on everything. Yet, at the same time, we observe the enormous pressure that the individual suffers to be the best in everything, the perfect synthesis of cultures, religions and beliefs, which results at its best in relativism and, at its worst, in indifference. Let us not forget how pervasive mockery is in our society, which is not necessarily a sign of good health and which tends to bring every issue down to the level of ridicule. From this, and from so many other aspects in our current world, each one us can witness to how close these tendencies are to us, in our family, at school, at home, and in the street.

Sometimes it occurs to us to say, quite spontaneously and without previous prejudice, "Our times are really bad. The whole human race is really evil." And without necessarily predicting the end of the world as "the day after tomorrow," we do not know very well at all where we're going.

What are we to do?

It doesn't help to dream, and nostalgia is not going to get us anywhere. The worst thing of all would be that we simply learn to accommodate and go along with the flow or that we let ourselves get locked into the system, never casting a critical or skeptical eye on the state of affairs. This world is our world. We cannot pretend that we just don't see it. There is no use in trying to take refuge in some ideal but vanished past. The world will simply not go back to those days. Besides, it still keeps on amazing us. Moreover, we cannot travel back in time with words or attitudes, or even with "methods" which were once effective but are useless today. On this point, Colin offers some guidance.

He tells us, "There's a pilot in the plane," or something that would sound like that in the pre-aviation imagery of his day. Do you remember the one who said "Yes" to the annunciation, thus allowing the birth of the Son of God into our world? She is the same one who said "Yes" to the crucifixion, accepting to become the mother of the disciple, then of the disciples, and then of the whole Church. And Mary is not going to abandon her children during their difficult moments. How could she turn away from the mission that Jesus entrusted to her?

Finally, Colin evokes Mary's place in the Church at its beginnings, drawing our attention to her role of uniting and binding. She disrupts nothing, she does not take one person's part against another, and she does everything without raising her voice. This attitude has become foundational for the Church, so that in any circumstance whatever, it is not by clever speeches or astounding actions that Mary is present, but in her silence and her interior attitude of trust and prayer.

Another look?

Mary at the beginning of the Church. Mary on the threshold of rebuilding the Church of the nineteenth century. Mary with us in our Church today. If we are to believe Colin, her presence can be the "pledge" of a "new Church." On condition, that is, that we leave everything up to her.

From this viewpoint, we should ask ourselves how we look at our times, our friends, our neighbors, our own children "who have totally given up the practice of religion," or "who have moved in together" apparently with no other thought than for the present moment, or "who are not getting their children baptized." From yet another angle altogether different but often just as painful, we hear of the son or daughter who converted to Buddhism, or the son who now lives with another man. There are many other painful experiences we could add to this litany, but, it runs the risk of growing longer and sometimes of assigning blame. Haven't we done everything we could to pass on our faith and our convictions to the younger generation? Certainly, we have. But is faith passed on like items in a will? And because the world is constantly changing, shouldn't the way we present the Gospel keep pace and change accordingly?

So will our look now be only suspicious? Will it go beyond surface impressions? Mary must teach us what she taught Jesus, to treat everyone as if he were unique, whether sinner or adulterer, whether leper or tax collector, etc. She teaches us as she taught him to discover the prostitute's real love, the Samaritan woman's real thirst. This obviously goes for everyone that Jesus met and loved.

Mary continues to tell us: Don't disrupt any-thing. Work for unity. Demand nothing except the Gospel. What do you know about what goes on in men's hearts? The grain of wheat grows forth in silence and patience, taking its time. God never asked us to make the grain grow, he just asked us to sow it.

Today, as in Colin's time, we have to come

up with an alternative to our way of living in the "world." And it cannot be only by resisting, but by trying to encounter others in their actual concerns and needs. Can we do this without clutching on to what we think we have to defend, or standing up out in front as the first ranks protecting and defending the besieged castle? Rather, can we live in a way that witnesses to a discreet God, who is often silent? And can we find the right place standing side-by-side with others, a place of listening and solidarity, there where the word is on the brink of touching hearts?

Reflection Questions

Today's reflection gives several examples of modern-day moral dilemmas. Can you explain in practical terms how you would try to apply the Christian principle "Hate the sin but love the sinner" to some of these dilemmas? How can Mary help us to grow in compassion and mercy toward those people who do not share our moral values? What are your strong talents in reaching the hearts of others? Could you use your talents to make another person feel accepted, appreciated, and even eager to share with you their spiritual and moral questions?

12
The Whole Universe

Focus Point

////////////

For more than a century, popular evangelism and
populist politics have promoted the ideal of equality, freedom, mutual respect and general harmony
among all people on the earth. Both preachers and
politicians have hailed a future when everyone
would recognize and embrace the "Brotherhood
of Man under the Fatherhood of God." Secular
and cynical reactions, at least in the United States,
labeled this quest as "BOMFOG," and employed it
in a most pejorative way. "BOMFOG" represents
any political platitude, unachievable and probably
a little crazy. In a critique of the underlying piety
and religious fervor, "BOMFOG" applies to any pie-
in-the-sky palliative creed as well as to the theory
of religion as opiate of the masses. But how do our
Christian teachings and values match up against
such criticism? At the very essence of our faith
lies the concept of "universal." Universal salvation

wrought in Jesus Christ, the Father's universal love of all creation, the *common* destiny of the *whole* human race, and the absolute equality of every single man, woman and child. Day 12 explores further ramifications of "the whole universe."

/////////////

You will be astonished to hear that I have a great ambition: to seize hold of the whole universe, under the wings of Mary by means of the Third Order. The Third Order is not an essential part of your congregation: but the blessed Virgin entrusts it to you like a bridge...to go to souls, to sinners. Never have the nations shown such eagerness to turn to the blessed Virgin, and at the end of time there will be only one kingdom, the kingdom of the blessed Virgin. (EK 85)

Seize hold of the universe?

Here we find an ambition that would make even Marists smile. For people who want to be unknown and hidden, what a claim! To seize hold of the whole universe, to be open to the entire world, to dream of the whole human race as being Marist, and even a Marist pope. About the pope, indeed. While he was meeting in Rome with a cardinal, Colin explained his plan. When His Eminence reacted surprised and asked Colin, "But then the whole world will be Marist?", Colin replied, "Yes, Eminence. Even the pope." What was this, a dream?

Megalomania? Wild imagination? Utopian fantasy? Of course, if it were anything like that, how could we justify putting this theme of "the whole world Marist" in this book?

To understand Colin's thinking, we have to remember his familiarity with Mary of Agreda, the Spanish visionary whose book, *The Mystical City of God,* he had read. We should also recall the connection that this nun makes between her visions and the Book of Revelation, particularly chapter 21. We read there the good news that, "God will dwell with them and they will be his people, and God himself will always be with them as their God." He will wipe every tear from their eyes, and there shall be no more death or mourning, wailing or pain, for the old order has passed away (Rev 21:3-4). For Mary of Agreda, the Virgin Mary, who gave birth to the Son of God and was at the birth of the early Church, will also give birth to that new world. It was this conviction that Colin took and made his own.

Some might find this naïve. But that would be to lose sight of the fact that this viewpoint, during Colin's time, showed bold courage. We have already recalled several times now the Church's rather rigid posture — the leftovers of Jansenism, the distrust toward heretics (Protestants, generally), and keeping one's distance from sinners. With a backstroke of his hand, Colin sweeps all that away and suggests that we stop for a moment before the Blessed Mother with her mantle widespread (this is a new image for Noah's ark). She shelters everyone in the folds of her garment, except, of course, for those who choose not to be there.

In the light of this vision, we can understand some of Colin's decisions better. For example, his accepting missions at the end of the known world, in the Southern Pacific, with all the resulting difficulties of access, relations with shipping lines, merchants, bishops, confreres, and all the follow up that we can only imagine. It seemed as if he were sending men and money out on mission, but without any return. Yet, after all, these "savages," as they were called then, were also totally and absolutely invited to salvation, and someone needed to tell them that.

Likewise, Colin did not choose particular ministries for his congregation. Of course, Marists had to prefer to go among the poor, but "the poor we always have with us." There were children to teach, the abandoned, prisoners, prostitutes, etc. Everyone has a place in the City of God, but still, someone has to invite them.

Summing up, Colin discovered that Christianity does not coincide with the "world" any more, and that the Church is far from being "universal." Thus, some people find comfort in letting themselves get wrapped up in questions of identity, while Colin draws a completely different conclusion. Let us reach out to "the world," that is, all the people who are near us or those who are far from us. Let us get closer to the ones who are farther away, and let us teach them the Good News that they do not yet know or that they do not know any longer.

A "catholic" Church

In Colin's plan, the Third Order occupies an important place which we will explain a little later. For now, we will stay with his vision. This Colinian "dream" can touch our hearts if we remember that we are "Catholics" and that every time we recite the Nicene Creed, we profess our belief in belonging to one, holy, catholic and apostolic Church. To call ourselves "catholic" of course means to give to the word its original sense of "universal" or "all-inclusive." Suddenly, the Apocalypse vision seems to loom on the horizon and we are heading toward it, and we are hoping to make it gradually become a reality.

We also know that the word "catholic" is sometimes used provocatively, a somewhat aggressive proclamation of identity, turned in on itself. In this sense, if something did not generally appear to be "Catholic," then many "good Catholics" would reject or condemn it.

To be a Catholic is to widen our outlook, expand our listening beyond the Sunday parish Mass. Naturally, we are no longer in Colin's place. He felt so urgently the need to carry the Gospel to people who had never before heard anything about it, or who had heard the Gospel preached but could no longer accept it the way it was presented to them. Our task in this twenty-first century may not be to go to the ends of the earth; the world has come to us now. We have to listen to what the people tell us about their hopes and aspirations and about their reasons for living. Without ruling anything out, we will often be surprised at their ways of "believing." Perhaps their questions, their comments, and even their challenges will confirm us in our own faith and prompt us to deepen it. And then we will also be able to explain to them our reasons for living and believing.

At the end of every Mass, the priest says, "Go in the peace of Christ." How do we understand that familiar phrase? As a friendly farewell meant to last the whole week, "Same time, same place, next Sunday"? Or is it an assignment, to "go out and serve your sisters and brothers."? At the end of Mass we have often sung, "Let us Build the City of God." And yet, we usually stay inside the Church, nice and warm.

Colin invites us to do something else. In his vision he takes the apostles' coming out from the upper room for the first time on Pentecost when they preached right there to people of the entire world. He unites that scene to what was happening in the background, where Mary was animating and encouraging the apostles in their first acts of ministry. The mother could wish only for the gathering and uniting of all her children. This is already a prefiguring of the great gathering announced in the book of Revelation. As we recall these images, each one of us could wonder, somewhat impertinently, "Can I truly call myself a Catholic? Am I concerned about the salvation of others? Am I ever amazed at other people's personal life story and find myself enriched by them?"

Colin invites us to the adventure of encounter. Perhaps it is a risk, but it's above all an opportunity. Let us reread some of the encounters Jesus had in the Gospel. Let us share his wonder at the Roman centurion's faith (Mt 8:10) or the faith of the Canaanite woman (Mt 15:28), or encountering the sinful woman's love (Mt 26:13) or the poor widow's generosity (Mk 12:43). We could add to this list all our own amazed and amazing encounters with those women and men who say that they do not share our Christian faith and yet who are already so close to the Gospel!

Reflection Questions

We understand the value of unity and harmony in a family. Are unity and harmony simply out of the question when it comes to a nation, or to politics, or to the market place and economics, or even to the Church? Is the human race cursed with division, distrust and selfishness? Can you think of times when you felt one with others in a large-group experience? How did that come about? Can you draw any lessons from those experiences to apply to our world today? How can you play a part in bringing about unity and harmony? Can you think of any idea or goal or common task that could possibly unite the human race?

13
A Tree with Four or Five Branches

Focus Point

////////////

Yesterday, for Day 12, we reflected on universality. Today we narrow our focus to the Society of Mary, particularly how Fr. Colin imagined one single religious order, with one Superior General, including priests, brothers and sisters, and even lay people. He was obviously naïve about explaining how the details of such a vast project would function. As we see things today, it was only natural that the Roman authorities told him to re-work his plan. In Day 13 we reflect on what resulted from Fr. Colin's re-thinking, while he still respected and valued the universality of the Marist charism.

////////////

[5] The Society, as conceived from the beginning and already active, as we said above, embraces several orders of religious: 1) the order of priests, 2) the order

of lay brothers, 3) the order of religious sisters, and 4) the confraternity of lay people living in the world.

[10] Those inscribed in the confraternity, however, take no vows, and they live in the world, but they observe certain exercises of piety, and thus, by their attachment to the Society, they become full participants in all the spiritual goods of the whole Society.

[110] Sinners may also be admitted, provided they are Catholic; for them to participate in the prayers and other spiritual goods of the Society, it is enough if their names are inscribed in the book of the confraternity kept by the religious priests of the Society of Mary. (LM 9)

///////////

A bountiful family

*T*he Marist project attracts people. At that time when battered French society was just beginning to catch its breath, the generation of thirty-year-olds did not lack for initiatives. We have already seen in our glance at the historical background how Marcellin Champagnat took to heart the education of young boys and so began to form his teaching brothers. We saw how Jeanne-Marie Chavoin and her friend Marie Jotillon, were attracted to the Marist project, then joined Jean-Claude Colin in Cerdon and, little by little, and often with difficulty and suffering, traced their own path. We also saw how, later, the incredible odyssey of Françoise Perroton would enrich the family of another branch, the Missionary Sisters of the Society of Mary.

Colin had foreseen that all this would be but one congregation, which Rome inevitably had to rule impossible. Thus it was that the individual groups became gradually more distinct from each other, yet maintaining the attitude and spirit of being one Marist family and always drawing inspiration from the same fountainhead.

The whole world Marist?

Here we could ask about the laity. Colin's boldness appears in the importance that he accords to lay people in the nineteenth-century Church. Naturally, there were some outstanding laymen and women who had the courage to speak up about this or that church issue. But they were the exceptions. Generally speaking, most of the clergy did not look with a favorable eye on any kind of lay initiative. One bishop said, "The mission of lay people is not to be concerned with Church affairs. Their duty is to pray."

In this context, Colin stands out conspicuously. The way in which he presents his project on the laity would have struck his contemporaries as way out of tune with current practice. For he gives the laity a completely original place in the Marist Family. He does not see lay people as the lower working levels of the Society of Mary; the laity does not orbit around the religious. The laity is not at the service of the religious, but rather, of the whole Church. Far from wanting to monopolize or rehabilitate the laity, Colin would like to make them available for the service of evangelization. The laity can be a bridge to reach out to souls! Colin underwent a telling debate with one of his closest collaborators, Fr. Peter Julian Eymard, the future founder of the Blessed Sacrament congregation. Eymard envisioned a third order that looked like a simplified, mini-religious order. Members were to call each other "brother" and "sister," and they would have a "superior." Within such a vision, he foresaw rather strict conditions for entry into the group, touching precisely on the candidates' religious dispositions and the quality of their interior life. Colin formally repudiated that whole structure. It should not be the purpose of the laity to resemble, even vaguely, "mini-religious." In that same vein, he did not hesitate to counsel lay groups *not* to meet in Marist houses, and he likewise suggested that diocesan parish priests mentor the laity. As explanation, it goes without saying that laymen and women are Christians, so they should live out their Christian lives in their parishes with their diocesan priests. As for recruiting new members, the field is practically unlimited. Only heretics are excluded.

A laity entirely apart

Times have changed, of course, and we cannot compare the laity's situation in the Church at Colin's time with our era. For a long time now, lay people have shown in countless ways how they fit into the Church, how they state their point of view, and how they work in the "world" as well as in the Church. On the other hand, priests and religious, like Mother Teresa of Calcutta and Abbé Pierre,[a] have shown only too well how they can shake up the world in the name of the Gospel. And that's wonderful. What remains for us now is to let Colin's ideas draw our attention to several specific points concerning the laity.

Notice the *confidence* he extends to the laity, and the irreplaceable role he entrusts them with.

See the *autonomy* that he recognizes for the laity in relation to the Marist religious congregation, which in no way hinders bonds of trust and love between lay people and religious.

---

a. Henri Marie Joseph Grouès, known as Abbé Pierre, 1912-2007, was an internationally famous French priest who fought for the Resistance during World War II and founded the Emmaus Movement (1949) helping the poor, homeless and refugees. He was involved all his life in social and political issues in France and elsewhere. [Translator's note]

Notice his awareness of a distinct *lay people*, which incorporates everyone who wants to be a part of it, without any discrimination, whether of age, gender, or condition, even welcoming children. We might pick up here a certain naïvety or a charming form of wishful thinking. But we can also detect in Colin's thinking a real understanding of what the People of God are. This is not just a group of friends or relations, but the very work of God, of The One who reconciles people with each other making them brothers and sisters as well as neighbors to one another, because of what Jesus Christ has done for each one of us.

Look at the *responsibility* that the laity has in evangelizing the world, and this they share with religious. Lay people are indispensable to religious, religious are indispensable to lay people.

The *fraternity* that Colin foresees is not, first of all, psychological or social. It is a spiritual brotherhood. It finds its origin in God's own desire. That is why the fraternity permits such an open company, including children, including sinners, including those who are apparently the farthest from the Church.

Are they bridges or barriers?

The story went around some time ago that a bishop asked the priests of his diocese never to welcome visitors with the question "Why?"

"Why are you looking at us?" "Why are you visiting us?" He asked the priests to say first of all, "I'm happy to see you, and I thank you for coming." Is this just some piddly little detail? Or is it a way of taking seriously the very simple matter of what joins us to each other, even before we get anywhere near to remembering that we have serious boundaries between us or recalling all the prohibitions and obligations our individual churches have decreed? Can this be a sign of recognizing, before anyone requests anything, our closeness to each other, the closeness that the Lord wants to establish among us all?

We believe in an incarnate God, Jesus, who during his stay with us on earth never ceased "to go and look elsewhere," to cross frontiers, to spend time in pagan villages, to meet people from a different race, from a different religion or from a different outlook on morality. He listened to them; he spoke to them. He sometimes healed them. He sometimes let his deep desire to gather all people together in order to save them slip out and be openly seen. And he invites us to be part of his mission. "Whatever you do to the least of these you do unto me."

A last word. In this beautiful initiative on the laity, Colin reserved for religious a not insignificant role. They are charged with the responsibility of forming these laymen and women in Marist spirituality.

It remains up to each one of us to examine our place in the Church such as Vatican II has called for, how we will exercise our responsibility as the baptized, how we will seek spiritual nourishment, where we will be nurtured so as to avoid fainting from hunger or from discouragement in our various commitments on our pilgrim way. It is also up to all to examine how they live in mutuality with the priests of the Society of Mary.

Reflection Questions

If you are a layperson, would you be willing to take a greater part in the mission of the Church – this includes spiritually, administratively, evangelizing and generally being "leaven" for the dough of the world? If you are a religious or cleric, do you think it appropriate for the laity to have greater roles in the Church? Whether you are a layperson or not, how do you see the laity growing in prayer, holiness, generosity, zeal and service? The very definition of a layperson is one living and working in the world, while at the same time living and growing in Catholic identity. Time pressures, the stresses of work and family obligations all impact on the typical layperson. Could you describe a minimum routine of Catholic life and practices that would be helpful, yet also realistic, for the laity?

14
Only Saints
Can Do Good

Focus Point

//////////////

These days we recognize that one of the most significant events in our lives and in the life of the Church has been the Second Vatican Council (1962–1965). Blessed John XXIII clearly hoped to throw open the Church's windows to let in the renewing grace of the Holy Spirit, and then use those same open windows for the Church to go out and engage the whole world, inviting everyone to embrace the Gospel. One of the great teachings of Vatican II is found in the Constitution on the Church, sometimes called by its Latin name, "*Lumen Gentium.*" Chapter 5 of that amazing document deals with the "universal call to holiness," that is, our belief that every single Christian, of whatever rank or status, is called, is expected, and is given every opportunity in life to be holy, to be a saint. And Chapter 5 demonstrates that this is not some far-off fantasy. Ordinary, every-day people can do it. A famous quotation from the 20th century, variously attributed to Jacques Maritain and his wife Raïssa, also to the French journalist Anton Péguy, as well as to the Catholic writer and mystic Léon Bloy, reminds us that "the only tragedy in life is not to become a saint."

///////////////

I am so mowed under that I have no time to think out what I should say to the confreres in Oceania, but I tell them all that they will not bear fruit except insofar as they march like the apostles to the conquest of souls. The apostles had left all things, they relied on nothing human, but on the grace and strength of their good master. Yes, and with that as their only help, they changed the world. Let us remind ourselves that we who remain in France are of the same family; we must, then, have the same spirit. And in France, I may tell you, we have just as much immorality, just as much evil as in Oceania. Only saints, then, can do good there — saints, that is to say, missionaries who will lead a life of sacrifice and of death. But we must die completely. You must be dead, not to learning, but to yourselves. (FS 160, 4)

///////////////

Everyone must be a saint?

" *B e saints!*" Colin launched this challenge to everyone. Certainly to his own confreres, the missionaries in Oceania, Marist candidates, lay people of the Third Order, private individuals whom he was spiritually mentoring, of whatever age in whatever social situation, he universally invited them to *"Be saints!"* as if it just went without saying. This might appear to us as simply a pious formula, as we might say today, "Good luck!" or "Take care of yourself." But not for Colin. For him, this invitation represents a program for life, a way of being and behaving.

We could imagine that many people who heard Colin saying this would have found it rather lovely, but would still be persuaded that he was speaking to others. And what about us? Should we move on right now to the next chapter? Maybe. But before doing that, it would be helpful to remember how St. Paul addressed Christians in the early communities. "Paul, to all the holy ones[a] throughout Achaia" (2 Cor 1:1). "You, then, God's chosen ones, holy and beloved ..." (Col 3:12). The subject here is about "ordinary" Christians, about whom we also know that they were not necessarily spiritual giants on some Olympian height or the moral

---

a. In earlier versions of the bible in English, the common translation for "holy" or "holy one" was "saint." [Translator's note]

pillars of their communities. Similarly, ordinary Christians, whether religious or not, are the people that Jean-Claude Colin addresses. And he also speaks to us today. What should we make of this title? How could we try to respond to it?

Colin considered it paramount to put his confidence in the right place. A saint commends his spirit entirely into God's hands and counts only on him in the manner of the first disciples sent on mission by Jesus. We remember that they carried nothing for the journey, except a walking stick. This path opens up a wide vista to everyone, no matter who it be, because right from the starting line nothing is required, except this confidence. We might hope to find support coming from our own talents, or from our relationships with others or from some means we have set in motion, but that self-sufficient approach only impedes our progress on the way to holiness and might even appear like some sort of defiance against God. That would be the worst thing of all.

For Colin, inviting is really a way of heartily inciting. An example can show us this. For a number of years, Fr. Colin was the spiritual mentor to a young man named Claude Mayet, who eventually became a Marist. As a lad, he suffered from a serious illness that rendered him mute, and which eventually turned into cancer. In a letter which Colin wrote him, Mayet read this advice:

Consider yourself just a bump on a log before
God. Speak to God as a child to its father.
Keep yourself in great peace like a child.

There definitely had to be great intimacy between the two of them to be able to say and receive such a profound message. Yet, at the same time, everything is said in only a few words: my own inability not only to do, but sometimes even to understand, what God is asking of me, as well as the recognition of what and who I am, and the discovery of God as father and the peace that flows from that. He also said to Mayet:

I want you to be a saint, a great saint.
(Colin.sup I, 33)

The Marists cannot count many canonized saints, only two in fact, St. Peter Chanel, martyr and patron of Oceania, and St. Marcellin Champagnat, founder of the Marist Brothers. Let us take a look at St. Peter Chanel. There is no doubt that Chanel heard and heeded his superior's recommendations. But his personal experience on the island of Futuna helped him to understand what he did not hear. His preparations and projections in France turned out to be worth nothing once he arrived in the South Pacific. In those three years, he never succeeded in learning the native language. He baptized a few babies and children and some old people in danger of death. And when he finally worked out a plan for evangelizing, he was assassinated because he was now getting in the way. Shortly after his death, the entire island converted, and the people began to call Peter Chanel "the man with the great heart." So, that is the result, the product, of someone who had nothing to work with, who could count on no one, not even his own gifts, and who came up with nothing, or very little. Nevertheless, people did remember this of him, "he loved the people." Saint Peter Chanel provided enough justification for Colin to write after the martyr's death:

He spent three years among the savages, as if in exile and in a fruitless ministry, and marked with so few conversions. (Colin.sup I, 337)

Saint Peter Chanel was not able to do anything, but he did let God do everything. He put his trust in God, and the conversions certainly followed.

To do and to let it be done

Talking about things on the other side of the world should not pull us away from our daily lives, on this side of the world. We, too, are familiar with a sense of impotence as we face tasks to accomplish or difficulties to surmount. We have all had the experience of discouragement, failure, maybe even "the night." What do we do then? How do we do it? How do we get ourselves out? At whatever our level, we live the passion which can be transformed into a fruitful passiveness if it is combined with the gift of ourselves, openness, and our consent and acceptance of whatever comes our way. Our times automatically equate productivity with efficiency, and they link efficiency to action. That is not Colin's method, and it is surely not the way the Gospel works. Let us imagine Colin holding two reins in his hands. One is action. God knows how hard he worked to send missionaries to Oceania, to find money, open new houses, teach the young, take interest in the affairs of the Marist Sisters and Brothers, and have dealings with Rome! The other rein represents welcoming others, preaching the fruitfulness of the grain of wheat that first dies and is buried hidden in the ground, and then hoping expectantly that others would trust him entirely "like children." Colin does not claim success for his actions when there is success, but he gives all the credit and thanks to the One who is the real author.

Colin, with his ambition to make saints of us, seems to be calling our bluff a little. Are *we* looking for results? Remember, that is not at all the essential thing for our lives.

Do we no longer understand "the will of God"? Colin simply asks us to accept it.

Have we thought of everything so as to come up with the results we desire? That's all right. But do we still think and believe that everything lies in the Lord's hands, and that our most sophisticated human preparations count for nothing if we do not spend equally as much time and effort on our prayer?

Would we be deeply disappointed by a failure, by a misunderstanding? But with failure and misunderstanding, we can always at least offer them to the Lord.

And we recall from St. Paul, "God chose us in him, before the world began, to be holy and without reproach" (Eph 1:4).

Reflection Questions

When we walk into church, say for Sunday Mass with the parish, it is easy to be conscious that we are all sinners in need of forgiveness and salvation ("Let us call to mind our sins"). How hard would it be to turn our focus totally around and adopt the New Testament vision, "Here are gathered *the saints* of St. X's parish"? Can you think of various ways that you are already a saint, or at least "holy"? How easy or hard would it be to look around the church on Sunday and see a gathering of saints? How does your attitude toward your fellow parishioners change? Can you learn from them, or be helped by them?

15
A New Church!

Focus Point

//////////////

Yesterday, we brought to mind the overwhelming grace that Vatican II was for the Church. We note that Pope John XXIII sincerely wanted to "update" the Church, which also means to renew the Church and even to reform the Church. As drastic as the word "reform" may sound, the Council reminded us on many occasions that quite an ancient axiom about the Church had always been accepted and implemented. "*Semper reformanda,*" that is, that the Church is always to be reformed or renewed. Since the Church is ever in flux and ever growing, at various historical moments the Holy Spirit inspires us to update, renew and reform the Church. Let us take that into account as we reflect on our last day, Day 15, on Fr. Colin's profound and heartfelt exhortation, "We much begin a new Church over again."

//////////////

The Society must begin a new Church over again. I do not mean that in a literal sense, that would be blasphemy. But still, in a certain sense, yes, we must begin a new Church. The Society of Mary, like the Church, began with simple, poorly-educated men, but since then the Church has developed and encompassed everything. We, too, must gather together everyone through the Third Order — heretics alone may not belong to it. (FS, 120, 1)

///////////////

Audacity or Folly?

"*B*egin a new Church over again!*" This sentence certainly gives us a jolt. And Colin does not tone it down much by emphasizing that it is not really revolutionary. Nonetheless, he insists, *"We must begin a new Church."* At the same time, he does maintain his viewpoint. He recommends adopting attitudes that we would not consider very "reformist" today, like absolute fidelity to the pope and obedience to bishops. If the Society of Mary is present in a bishop's diocese, he should be able to consider it as if it were his own religious order. Marists are to exercise discretion even up to seeming invisible in diocesan parishes so as not to offend the parish priests. They should not engage in debate over doctrine or pastoral practice, and they will yield their place to other congregations if these latter want to take it!

So, what exactly does Colin want? He has organized his project between two reference points. The first one is the state of the Church when Marist religious life was beginning. He encountered a Church dilapidated and dismantled. The second is the vision of the new-born Church, at Pentecost, around the charter members, Mary and the apostles. In the dynamic between these two images Colin thought through and identified a new Church. Here are some traits it is supposed to display, traits that were essential for him.

First of all, a new Church must *point back to the origin*, to Pentecost, the pouring out of the Holy Spirit. Just as the Messiah is born from the outpouring of the Spirit overshadowing Mary at the Annunciation, so the first community of the Church is born from the Spirit descending at Pentecost. We must not so much remember this as an historical event, but as an event that continues to occur in our times, in our world, in our Church and in our lives. The Church is not the goal of some project or construction of ours. She comes to the light of day and endures wholly in the Holy Spirit. And to keep living she must let the Spirit breathe within her depths down all her days and let him, in a way, fertilize or fructify all her actions.

According to Colin's vision, *the Church gathers together.* We can see in this position the exact opposite of the Church of the Ancien Regime[a] and even of a political system which discriminates, justifying differences and inequalities. Colin can find no limits to gathering people in. For him it is not enough to go to the frontiers, but we must push on far beyond geographically, socially, and pastorally, that is, go beyond people who already identify themselves as Christian. We might even get the impression that the farther away from the Church someone is, the more Colin makes him the object of his interest.

And to attain this second goal, we have to *adapt our language and our methods.* "Hidden and unknown," as we have seen, is not meant to be a moral guideline, nor is it a strategy for someone to infiltrate the world like a mole working deep cover in a spy network. At the same time, this phrase implies an understanding of the inner workings of our secular and unbelieving world, and a solidarity without reservation, almost an osmosis, with all those whom we will encounter in the world. On this point, Marists should entertain a little misgiving about themselves because they can easily become, consciously or not, obstacles to the encounter, to the gathering

---

a. "Earlier Order," a term referring to the ensemble of monarchy, aristocracy, government, church and society which functioned in the centuries before the French Revolution (1789-1799). One of the aims of the Revolution was to abolish the "*Ancien Régime.*" [Translator's note]

in, to the proclamation. They might do this by the positions they take, by their language, by their desire to step up on the stage with some kind of "look-at-me" behavior, or by unacceptable chatter. There are so many obstacles that we can build between people and the Good News. And we really do want to proclaim it, the Good News, not ourselves. This is also a valid message for all those in the Church or elsewhere whose mission it is to listen, to mentor and to welcome.

The consequence of such a process is to sweep any *institutional concerns* into the background. It's not so much that the Church has to endure for eternity as to begin again humbly every morning, persevering in prayer and in the breath of the Spirit. The Church, according to this vision, thinks of herself as wanting to do everything for others and not, first of all, for herself. She is servant more than mistress, and claims no privileges. She is a Church that listens more than teaching what is right, what is wrong, and what you have to believe. She is a Church that abandons defense positions and pretensions to privilege. This is a Church whose only concern is to proclaim Jesus. She does not reject being fragile, for she sees in fragility even the sign of good spiritual health, of an open door to the Holy Spirit so that he can come in and feel free to do as he chooses.

To sum up, this new Church is a Church always in process of being "begun over again," and it is always being built up on a wonderful union of hearts and the great rejections that Colin pronounced against cupidity in all its forms of pride, and the lust for power and the desire for show.

Begin a new Church over again

To begin a new Church over again — is that a valid goal for today? In Colin's time the Church certainly suffered grave difficulties. As a message and as a promise, he received this "revelation" from Mary:

She was the support of the Church in the first times, she will be so as well at the end. (EK 14)

Strengthened by this assurance, he gave life to a religious family. In a society that was sorely afflicted and in a devastated Church, Colin and the first Marists found the way to go forward, to preserve and give back hope to Christians, and to proclaim the Gospel. And they did this by keeping in their hearts the image of the early Church.

Today, can this same "revelation" produce new life and enthusiasm in us?

Will we share Mary's love for life? Will we proceed "in haste" to the place where life is born, rather than weep over what has been disappearing or dying?

Will we be convinced that the Holy Spirit of Pentecost has more to tell us than do diminishing numbers and figures in the red — convinced that we would do much better to spend more time with that Spirit than to dwell on those negatives?

Will we believe that the Church, as a mother, never accepts a report card of final failure for even one of her children, but that she is always prepared to hope, because she is his mother, and he is her child? Do we believe that because she has many children, that she eagerly desires to save them *all*?

Will the Gospel we proclaim be Good News? Will people believe that the God who is proclaimed to them is not horrified or hurt by their limitations, but that he looks upon them with benevolence, just as a mother looks lovingly on her children at the same time that she can accurately recognize their weaknesses and flaws?

Our age, after all, could also easily be the age of Mary, as Colin considered his era. Specifically, that is an age when people really need to discover a counterbalance to the frenzy of the world and the drive to master everything and everyone. One look at our age confirms that success has replaced salvation or made it obsolete! And then there is Mary, more concerned with attentiveness than with action, more interested in silence than in speech, with her real presence than with media coverage.

Mary is alive and well in the Church of our times. She is in our midst, as in early times, always listening to the Holy Spirit. Let us turn toward her, for she would have us deeply understand and love and care for the Church.

Reflection Questions

Trying to be both objective and charitable, can you list places and ways our Church needs to be "begun over again" in Fr. Colin's expression, or renewed and revitalized in today's language? Think of the Universal Church, the diocese, the parish, etc. In what ways do *you* need to be renewed to be a better Catholic and a more effective disciple? In our quest for renewal, personal and collective, what are the benefits of looking back to the ideal time of the new-born Church, at Pentecost and with Mary's presence?

For Further Reading

Stanley W. Hosie, S.M. *Anonymous Apostle: the Life of Jean-Claude Colin, Marist.* William Morrow & Company. New York, 1967.

Donal Kerr, S.M. *Jean-Claude Colin, Marist, a Founder in an Era of Revolution and Reformation: the Early Years 1790–1836.* The Columba Press. Dublin, 2000.

Craig Larkin, S.M. *A Certain Way, an Exploration of Marist Spirituality.* Marist Publications. Rome, 1995.

Jan Snijders, S.M. *The Age of Mary.* Marist Publications. Rome, 1998.

Also available in the
"15 Days of Prayer" series:

Saint Benedict *(André Gozier)*
978-1-56548-304-0, paper

Saint Bernadette of Lourdes *(François Vayne)*
978-1-56548-314-9, paper

Dietrich Bonhoeffer *(Matthieu Arnold)*
978-1-56548-311-8, paper

Saint Catherine of Siena *(Chantal van der
Plancke and Andrè Knockaert)*
978-156548-310-1, paper

Pierre Teilhard de Chardin *(André Dupleix)*
978-0764-804908, paper

Saint Vincent de Paul *(Jean-Pierre Renouard)*
978-1-56548-357-6, paper

The Curé of Ars *(Pierre Blanc)*
978-0764-807138, paper

Saint Dominic *(Alain Quilici)*
978-0764-807169, paper

Saint Katharine Drexel *(Leo Luke Marcello)*
978-0764-809231, paper

Don Bosco *(Robert Schiele)*
978-0764-807121, paper

Saint Clare of Assisi *(Marie-France Becker)*
978-1-56548-371-2

Charles de Foucauld *(Michael Lafon)*
978-0764-804892, paper

Saint Francis de Sales *(Claude Morel)*
978-0764-805752, paper

Saint Francis of Assisi *(Thaddée Matura)*
978-1-56548-315-6, paper

Saint Jeanne Jugan *(Michel Lafon)*
978-1-56548-329-3, paper

Saint Eugene de Mazenod *(Bernard Dullier)*
978-1-56548-320-0, paper

Henri Nouwen *(Robert Waldron)*
978-1-56548-324-8, paper

Saint Martín de Porres: A Saint of the Americas *(Brian J. Pierce)*
978-0764-812163, paper

Meister Eckhart *(André Gozier)*
978-0764-806520, paper

Thomas Merton *(André Gozier)*
978-1-56548-330-9, paper

Saint Elizabeth Ann Seton *(Betty Ann McNeil)*
978-0764-808418, paper

Brother Roger of Taizé *(Sabine Laplane)*
978-1-56548-349-1, paper

Saint Teresa of Avila *(Jean Abiven)*
978-1-56548-366-8, paper

Saint Thérèse of Lisieux *(Constant Tonnelier)*
978-1-56548-391-0

Saint Thomas Aquinas *(André Pinet)*
978-0764-806568, paper